HOW TO WRITE YOUR FIRST BOOK

A BLUEPRINT FOR FICTION & NON-FICTION WRITERS

Stefanie Newell

Write One Publications, Inc.

MARIETTA, GA

Stefanie Newell/Write One Publications
www.howtowriteabookthatsells.com

How To Write Your First Book/ Stefanie Newell. – 2nd ed.

Additional books from Stefanie Newell

Overcoming The Fear Of Writing

Before The Writing: How To Do Research

Video Courses:

How To Write Your First Book video course

Available at http://howtowriteabookthatsells.com

CONTENTS

SO YOU WANT TO BE A WRITER?................................... 1

THE NUTS & BOLTS OF WRITING 11

CATERING TO YOUR TARGET AUDIENCE................. 37

SELF-PUBLISHING VS. TRADITIONAL PUBLISHING 41

THE BLUEPRINT FOR SUCCESS.................................. 51

HOW TO MARKET YOUR FIRST BOOK 59

YOUR VERY FIRST BOOK LAUNCH........................... 61

WHAT ARE YOUR GOALS AS A WRITER?.................. 79

WHAT IS YOUR COMFORT LEVEL?............................ 85

GETTING STARTED ON YOUR MARKETING PLAN... 87

THE PRESS RELEASE.. 91

GARNERING PUBLICITY FOR YOUR TITLE 93

TRADITIONAL MARKETING FOR WRITERS 97

BLOGGING AND THE AUTHOR................................... 103

WRITERS AND SOCIAL MEDIA 107

FINAL THOUGHTS 113

SO YOU WANT TO BE A WRITER?

Writing a book can be a very intimidating process for a first time author. It's for that reason that many people don't get any further than their idea, for fear of the process being too overwhelming. Writing and publishing can be such a steep learning curve that many of the resources available can leave you more confused than when you started. Although well intentioned, a few months of research can leave aspiring writers still wondering, how do I get started? How do I choose a topic? How do I outline? How long should my book be? Should I self-publish or traditionally publish?

But what if I could provide you with a blueprint that you could use over and over again that will help you to navigate this process quickly and more efficiently? Would that be helpful to you and take you from talking about writing to actually writing?

There are many different types of writers and this book will be helpful for each of you. Perhaps you are a fiction writer with an idea for a novel or a non-fiction writer who's an expert on a particular subject matter and is looking to take your business to the next level or looking to extend your brand with a book. What you will read on the forthcoming pages will provide you with more confidence to begin writing.

This book is written as a simple and easy to use blueprint for the newbie writer who doesn't have a clue how to get started. This book is meant to answer those questions you're too afraid to ask or questions that may seem simplistic in nature, but vital to beginning your writing career.

Because writing and publishing are likely new journeys you're embarking upon, I want you to be armed with as much information as possible, without overwhelming you and sending you screaming for the hills. While this book will encourage you to finish your manuscript as quickly as possible, this book isn't about speed. I won't sell you on writing your book in seven days, because let's face it you're a newbie. Because you are learning, the process may take a bit longer. But what if you could write your first book in six months and it is something you're absolutely proud of? Is that something you can aspire to do?

Yes? Then perfect.

Just to be clear, this book isn't about the writing itself. There are many books that can provide you with in-depth information on the writing process. Instead, what I will share is how to go from having a great concept for a book to being published. I want to share this information with you because at one point I was you – a newbie writer with no idea how to get started.

Writing has always come naturally to me. However, when I first started writing I had no clue about getting my ideas in a proper format on my computer, how long it should take to write a manuscript, how to get an agent, or even how to market it. I could go on and on, but you get the point. I was clueless about everything. Once I had it all figured out, I wondered why there weren't more resources that made it simple.

So I will be the change I seek to see in the world and share both my challenges and successes in hopes that you will use this blueprint to create, write, and publish your first book. Purchasing this book was your first step towards becoming a published author and for that you should be extremely proud.

By reading this book you'll learn how to:

- Affirm you are a writer
- Choose a genre
- Establish the name you will write under
- Research your book idea
- Beat writer's block
- Make time to write
- Format your manuscript
- Determine how long your book should be
- Cater to your target audience; and
- Choose between self-publishing and traditional publishing

Making The Decision To Write

A commonality I find among aspiring writers is their fear to proclaim themselves as a writer, or their fear to take the first step and actually commit to writing. I am going to encourage you to let go of that fear. Fear is paralyzing and will hinder you from making any forward momentum. If I had a dollar for every person who's told me they had an idea for a book, yet they never started a manuscript, I'd be a millionaire!

"What ifs" are a hindrance to creativity and will prevent you from ever becoming a published author. Affirm that you are an author and that you will complete your book within six months and then work toward that goal with fervor.

There are many reasons why people don't claim the title of author. For some, they know that staking claim to the title requires them to actually write and that may be a bit intimidating. For others it may be the stigma that goes along with writing. The image often portrayed in the media is the nerdy reclusive writer who makes very little money.

I often tell the story of the very first book festival I attended. I had so much enthusiasm about my new writing career. As I sat at my table with my books stacked and ready for my first customer, I had nothing but high hopes for my debut release. As I sat waiting, an established author walked up to my table.

"Is this your first book?" she asked.

"Yes, yes it is," I answered proudly.

I had a feeling that she'd been writing for some time, so I asked, "What about you?"

"I've written over 20 books," she said.

Hoping she would provide some guidance and wisdom, I peppered her with a few more questions, to which she adamantly responded, "If you plan to make money from writing books, then you've chosen the wrong career."

While her comment didn't deter me from pursuing writing, I was very put off by her candor.

Obviously it didn't stop me from pursuing a writing career, however, there are many aspiring writers who are told this and they become deterred. It stops many from seeking to write full-time, or even part-time for that matter.

If what has deterred you from writing has anything to do with financial compensation, there is some truth to what the author shared. However, as a published author and now a book coach there are a few things that I can share with you with respect to the monetary aspect of writing that may be helpful. These are things that this veteran author didn't share with me that I wish she had.

Writing is obviously a creative undertaking. It requires a time investment, just like any other career path you're embarking on. Much like going to school for a trade, you'll need to go to school for writing (so to speak). Whether you choose to actually participate in writing and publishing courses, read books such as this, or use Google as your school of choice, there is a learning curve that will require your time. It's for that reason that you'll have to allow time for your career to blossom.

Be honest with yourself about what is required for writing to be your full-time career, and then give yourself time to make it happen. Being a successful published author is not a goal that will happen overnight.

Prior to making the decision to write professionally, I worked for some of the biggest financial companies in the United States. Monday through Friday I would sit at my desk and oversee millions of dollars for my clients and every two weeks I would get a check that reflected my work. Though challenging in the beginning, after some time the work became easier. I could oversee the money in my sleep.

Writing is a bit different! Whether you write fiction or non-fiction it requires you to be creative and present, and in most cases you write without knowing whether you will be compensated fairly in the end. That's why I encourage writers to really ask themselves; is writing my passion? Is this the career I would choose whether I were being compensated or not? If you answer yes to both of those questions, then it will be during those days when you're writing your first draft and not being compensated for your time that your passion will propel you forward.

After I embarked upon my writing career, I had a friend share with me that she'd decided she was quitting her job and going on sabbatical to write her first book. At this point, I had been away from my corporate job for about two years and I knew what that path consisted of.

My first advice to her was to make sure she'd acquired a nice savings before she made the decision to walk away. You'd be surprised how quickly a savings dries up when you don't have any income. The second thing I suggested was for her to be stingy with her time. There's something about working from home that makes people assume you're sitting around watching reality shows while snacking on bonbons.

Friends and family will begin to ring your phone incessantly. The requests to do them a quick favor will become a part of your everyday routine, and before long you'll realize that you've wasted your entire day and haven't written a thing.

While I will talk about this more in an upcoming chapter, I actually wrote my first book while working a full-time job, blogging, freelancing, going to school, and being a mother. If it's at all possible for you to maintain your day job, I would encourage you to do so. That way, you won't have the financial pressure you would have if you quit.

With that being said, here's what I wish I were told by the veteran author.

Nothing sells your first book like a second book, and nothing sells your third book like your first two books. When I first published my book, I had great success. However, even with that success I still didn't live up to the numbers I thought I would in that first year. Because of that, I became paralyzed and stopped writing in hopes that I would figure out where I went wrong and to determine why I didn't hit my projected numbers. It took me a minute, but at some point I realized that I'd made a mistake in not continuing to write! I was a new writer with no fan base, and like all the writers that came before me, I needed to establish myself first.

My experience was not unique to me. There are countless other writers who feel like they didn't make enough money with their first book and they do just as I did and stop writing. However, if you look at the writers who are truly successful, they have lots of books on the market. If you are seeking to write as a career, then you'll need to do exactly that – write!

Write enough books so that you can be a success. Writing one book and quitting because you didn't recoup costs or because you didn't make as much as you thought you would, will not put you in a position to be successful.

Lastly, be realistic! This is extremely important.

I was able to pursue my passion for writing because I was laid off from my cushy corporate position. If it weren't for that, I don't know that I would have had the courage to step out on faith and pursue this career full-time as I've done. Did it take a level of courage to not go and find another corporate position? Well yes, on some level it did. However, I will say that faith has pushed me a good portion of the way.

If I were being totally transparent, I would share that it has taken me a number of years to secure a comfortable lifestyle. It's not quite the lifestyle I had as an analyst, but am I comfortable? Absolutely.

If I continue to write, my potential to increase my income expands. I project that the more I write, it will be possible to exceed the income I made as an analyst. Also, I'm much happier than I ever was in my corporate position! Writing and helping people is my purpose and it brings me great joy. You can't put a price tag on that!

So what allows an author to be comfortable?

In addition to receiving an income from writing books, it's important to supplement your income.

Despite being a great writer, success still takes time. Sure, we've heard of the overnight success stories. These are the people who decided they needed to make a few thousand dollars a month, they then sit down to their computer and crank out a bestseller. But the majority of us will have to work a little harder to make that happen. So I encourage you to think about additional ways you can add to your income.

I supplement my income in a few ways. Aside from books, a good bulk of my income comes from my book consulting business where I coach writers just like you to success. I also have several smaller streams of income.

First I started a blog. Originally I created my blog as a way to build my fan base and promote my book consulting business, but it also helped me to gain passive income through advertising. I started a YouTube channel, which again allows me to grow my fan base, promote my business, and I also receive advertising revenue from this medium as well. I also have video courses for writers that provide me with an additional source of income.

In addition to the books I sell on Amazon, I also have books that are exclusive to my personal websites. Because I'm my only competition on my website, I'm able to charge according to the value of my books and not by what everyone else is charging on Amazon. Lastly, I make money from doing speaking engagements.

Think outside of the box! How can you create additional streams of income as it relates to your niche or genre?

As a non-fiction writer, feel free to use the aforementioned ideas as ways you can make additional money. As a fiction writer, you will be able to do a few of these, but it will be very important for you to simply continue writing.

If you know that writing is your passion and what you seek to do whether full or part-time, commit to it today. Be realistic in your goals and give yourself ample time to allow it to manifest. Give yourself permission to make mistakes, but more importantly, produce quality work. In the next chapter, I will discuss the importance of good quality writing and how it's vital to your success, along with how to get your ideas out of your mind and onto your computer.

CHAPTER ONE

THE NUTS & BOLTS OF WRITING

Before I get into the fundamentals of writing a book, I want to address a question that I get asked often. What's the difference between fiction and non-fiction? While this may be obvious for some, I realize that it can be confusing for others. So because of this I just want to go over this briefly so that you can be sure which you write.

Fiction – Novels, Novellas, Short Stories

- Fiction works include made-up characters and a made-up series of events, called the plot. In addition to the main plot a novel may contain one or more subplots.
- Fiction also includes conflict and setting.
- Fiction is told from a certain perspective or point of view.
- Works of fiction often include a theme or message about life.

Non-Fiction - Biographies, Autobiographies, Informational Texts, etc.

- A title that engages your target audience.
- Well-written, factual information.
- The writer is an expert (or has extensive experience) in the field or subject matter.
- The material is well organized.
- Non-fiction deals only with real people, events, or ideas.
- Narrated from the point of view or perspective of the author, who is a real person.

The above should give you a clear understanding of the difference between the two.

My writing career actually began with fiction. I had no idea that I would write so many non-fiction books. However, the more I wrote, the more non-fiction came just as natural to me as fiction. As long as you are focused and writing quality content, I believe it is entirely possible to write in both genres (more on this in the next section).

However, for the sake of your first project and building your brand as a writer, I suggest that you make a decision about which genre you'll establish yourself in first.

So for your first manuscript, which of these genres will you write? Fiction or non-fiction?

What's In A Pen Name?

After you've made the decision to write fiction or non-fiction, the next thing you need to consider is what name you'll write under. Obviously a lot of writers use their actual name, but there are unique situations where authors decide to use a pen name. I've listed a few of these reasons below.

- You don't want people to know you write.
- Another author owns your name.
- You're writing in a genre different than your usual and you don't want to confuse your target audience.
- The subject of your book could potentially interfere with your full-time job.
- You're writing about sensitive topics such as: erotica, or books of a political or religious nature.
- You have a first or last name that's pretty difficult to spell and you feel that it will be difficult for readers to find you in search engines or on Amazon.
- You have an idea for a really marketable author name and you think it will work better than your own name.
- You are a male or female and writing in a genre that's common for the opposite sex.
- You want to try writing in a new genre and you don't want to be judged for it by your current fan base.
- Your name doesn't fit the genre you write in.

When I published my first book, I thought it was the most absurd thing in the world to write under any name other than my own. As hard as I'd worked on my manuscript I wanted the world to know that I'd written that book! I didn't want anyone else to take credit for a book that I'd worked blood, sweat and tears to produce.

However, that was a newbie mindset. Fast forward some years later and I fully understand why people write under pen names and as a result I now write under a few.

Many of us have numerous ideas we'd like to write about. What if you have a bunch of ideas and they don't all relate to the same target audience? For instance, what if you have an idea for a romance book and a children's book? Clearly these are two different demographics.

I'm not sure why this is (and I don't personally subscribe to this theory), but in the publishing industry readers really want you to stick to one genre. If you write fiction they want you to only write fiction. If you write non-fiction they don't want you to dabble in children's books. Now when you sit back and think about this, it's understandable on some level! However, if you look at it objectively, who in the world is only good at one thing?

Most of us have extensive knowledge of a lot of different subjects and multiple talents.

For instance, I worked in corporate finance for over 15 years and my bachelor's degree is in finance. Right before I graduated from college, I was required to write an extensive paper on personal credit. At about 100 pages I handed the paper off to my advisors to review. They were all extremely impressed with the information I'd shared and each of them expressed that they themselves had learned something from reading it. All of them held master's degrees and PhDs. Surely this information could be beneficial to someone just leaving their parents home and getting started with their personal credit, couldn't it?

I haven't done so yet, but I think that paper would make a great book!

The point is...writing under a pen name has its advantages, if not for any other reason than to avoid confusing your target audience. It also gives you a sense of freedom. Sure, it will sting if you receive a bad review or a less than stellar comment, but you'll be less concerned about what people think if you don't have your friends, family and peers watching.

With that being said, writing under a pen name is not an excuse to publish subpar writing. After all, it still requires the same time and financial investment as writing a book in your own name. You are still building a brand under the name and you should treat it accordingly.

Stay true to the pen name you choose! Let's say you're a woman and you've decided that you're going to write under a male pen name. For all intents and purposes, you're a man! Your audience sees you as a man and has no idea that you're writing under a pen name. So write as he would write, express ideas the way he would. Think of it as creating a character - become him!

There are also some disadvantages to writing under a pen name as well. The whole idea of a pen name is to be anonymous.

Pen names will inhibit you from doing speaking engagements, book signings, and in person interviews. It will also hinder you from being able to share with your friends and family that the #1 bestseller they're raving about is in fact you.

Pen names will always brand you as the elusive writer who doesn't share photos on social media. However, there are ways to use this mystery to your advantage and you should consider this while branding yourself.

Lastly, be mindful of the pen name you choose. Choose a name that's not too generic and obvious! Do research to ensure that the name is not that of another established author and be mindful of including your pen name on copyright forms and letters to agents. Seek legal counsel with respects to any tax implications and when signing publishing agreements.

Using a pen name is a personal decision and not necessary for every writer, however it is available in the event that you seek to conceal your identity.

How Do I Get Started?

When I was first asked this question it honestly threw me for a loop. My initial thought was, "Well just start writing." But after I had time to reflect on the question, I realized that it's just not that simple. There is a strategy that you can employ that will help set you up for success.

So let's start with the basics. While you likely may have a few book ideas that are nagging at you, pick one. If you find yourself saying, "There's this fiction book I want to write and there's also this memoir. Oh and how could I forget the children's book I want to write?" Get focused! In my experience, many aspiring writers never seem to get focused enough to start on any of the ideas.

Choose the one idea that you're the most passionate about. Remember, all of those other ideas will come to fruition at a later time, but first you need to start with the one that is going to keep you motivated to write. If you're just so-so about an idea, at some point it will reflect in your time and attention to the book. So give it some thought, what is that book idea for you?

Now that you have your idea, you'll need to do research to determine if there's a market and whether that market is profitable. This is beneficial for fiction books, but especially important for non-fiction books.

I've had some non-fiction books that I was really excited about writing. However, once I did the research I discovered that there really wasn't a big enough audience for me to devote my time to it.

So how do you determine profitability? You go to the biggest book search engine of them all – Amazon.com.

Let's say you're a photography enthusiast and you want to write a Kindle book about Canon cameras. It would be wise to go to Amazon and put "Canon cameras" into the search box, choose the 'Kindle Store' from the drop down menu and see what books show up in the search. (Note: If you are publishing a print book choose the 'Books' option from the drop down menu instead). At the time of this writing, when I enter the term "Canon cameras" a total of 132 books show up.

At first glance, 132 books may be promising because it could mean that there isn't a huge amount of competition. Or on the other hand, it could mean that there's not a big enough demand. Let's dig into this further and see if this is a good niche to write about.

When you put a search term in Amazon, it will show 16 results per page. The books that are doing the best will show up on page one among these 16 results. These are the results we care about, because let's face it, when people put "Canon cameras" into the search box you want your book to show up on page one. The further back in the search you show up, the less likely you are to be discovered.

Once you have your 16 results, click on the first book and go into the book's page as if you were going to purchase the book. Scroll down past the book description until you get to the section called product details. Once there, you're looking for the Amazon's Best Sellers Rank. Keep in mind you want to do this for each and every book among your 16 results.

A good sales ranking will be low. For example, a book that has a sales ranking of 1 is doing awesome and is a bestseller. Whereas a book that is in the millions isn't doing as well. Bear in mind that sales ranking can vary by hour and by day, and depending on how vast a category is, this can affect the sales ranking as well. That doesn't mean the fluctuation is significant. It just means that a book could rank at number 1 in the morning and then number 5 later in the afternoon depending on how many books were sold.

When researching a book idea, I'm looking for a niche where a fair amount of the first 16 results show a 100,000 sales rank. So now you're probably asking why 100,000 Stefanie?

100,000 is the gauge I use for determining whether I want to write about a certain topic. The reason I use this as a gauge is because it means that these books are selling fairly well. After all, who wants to write a book in a genre or niche where they are only selling 1 or 2 copies a month?

When I look at the first 16 book results around the keyword "Canon cameras," I find that quite a few of these books have a sales ranking higher than 100,000, which tells me that this isn't a topic I'd want to write a book about. When I further reflect on the number of books that showed up in the search (in this case it was 132) I know that this is because there just isn't a high demand.

Now I want to say a few things. First, this isn't a science. I repeat, this isn't a science! Nothing about this is perfect.

However, it's beneficial to have an idea of how well you can expect your book to do.

Obviously there are some passion projects we take on, where we're like, "Well even if it helps one person, that's all I truly want." And that's fine if that's how you choose to go about finding the topic you write about. However, just know that if you write a book in a niche that's not very popular, it will affect your sales.

Because there are so many books being published to Amazon daily, it will be hard to find a perfect niche or genre.

There will be certain instances where you may choose to throw caution to the wind and just get in there and compete! I did this with my first two books, mainly because I just didn't know any better. Now that I've been a published writer for quite some time, I wouldn't write a book without first doing a bit of research.

For fiction writers you have it a little easier. Much of what people will be searching for on Amazon will be around the genre you write. So when you're putting keywords in the search box you would put in keywords like romance, mystery thriller, historical fiction and things like this. You could also put in keywords around your character or the theme of your book. For example, if your main character is a serial killer, put "serial killer" into the search box.

Whether you are a fiction or non-fiction writer, don't just stop at one keyword; choose several to ensure that you aren't ruling out an idea too early! Let's go back to the "Canon cameras" example again. What if you put in the keyword, DSLR. Would that produce better results? Keep at it until you find the perfect niche that goes with your book idea.

Lastly, every book doesn't have to be sold on Amazon. Ideally you do want your book to be sold on Amazon because they are the largest book retailer and have a large customer base, but every successful author is not made on Amazon alone. There are many other sites where you can sell your book including your own website or blog. I have a book that I wrote a while back where I felt the genre was too competitive on Amazon. So instead, I put the book on my own website because I received good traffic and I knew that every single person visiting my website was looking for information on this topic. And guess what? The book did well.

The whole point of this exercise is to help set you up for success. Forgoing this step doesn't make it impossible for your book to do well. However, with such a huge time investment and, in some cases, a financial investment, wouldn't you want to give your book the best chance at success?

And one last thing... just because a niche or genre is over saturated doesn't mean that your book can't compete. That's where awesome writing and book marketing comes into play! You can learn about book marketing in the second book in this series, *How To Market Your First Book*. And just as an FYI, don't wait until you're done writing before you start thinking about marketing. These two things should be done concurrently.

Honing Your Book Idea

Now that you know that you are writing in a profitable niche or genre, how do you bring your book idea to fruition? The first thing you need to do is come up with additional ideas for your book.

If you are a fiction writer and you want to write a book about a woman who is betrayed, what kind of betrayal will it be? And how will she discover it?

There are numerous ways to come up with additional ideas for your plot. The first place to look is within your own life. Has something interesting happened in your life or in the lives of your family and friends that could be adapted for fiction? What about something you saw on the news? On the Internet? In a movie? Or a television show?

Have you heard the saying that there is nothing new under the sun? It's true - especially as it relates to books! With that being said, you don't want to blatantly rip off someone's idea. Instead you want to bring a fresh and interesting perspective to a plot that's been done time and time again. People have been betrayed in books since the beginning of time. What fresh perspective can you bring to your book that won't make your book seem like the same rehashed story?

The same goes for your characters. Have you run into a person, maybe at a grocery store that was a protagonist waiting to happen? Or perhaps your spouse has some really annoying quirks that would work well for your antagonist?

Consider all of this when coming up with ideas for your plots and characters.

If you're a non-fiction writer and you want to write a book for people just graduating from college and entering the workforce, what kinds of questions would this person have? What advice can you provide that will be beneficial for them? What problem can you solve for them?

You already know a little about this demographic. You know that they are both male and female and can be anywhere from 22 years of age or older. You know that they are obviously college educated. What additional details can you find out about them? What magazines do they read? What websites do they visit? What are their concerns as it relates to finding a job? Are they concerned about their social media footprint? Are they interested in internships?

Knowing this information is important. Visiting the same websites as your target audience will allow you to be a part of their world. Observe the topics they discuss and the questions they ask around the subject matter you are writing on. If you observe a question coming up over and over again, make sure you address that question in your book.

The next thing you can do is go back to Amazon and look at those first 16 results that pop up around the keyword you entered. Read both the good and bad reviews of those books. This will help you to determine what other writers did well and help you to determine the areas in which the authors were lacking. If for instance you see reviewers mentioning over and over again that a particular author didn't address how beneficial LinkedIn is for college graduates, then don't you think this is something you should highlight in your book?

If you really want to go above and beyond, read at least the first two or three books that show up in the results. Note the author's writing style, how they set up their chapters, their pacing, etc. If that seems like too much, then I would caution you to rethink the educational component required for writers. Good writers are avid readers!

I get it! We all get busy and sometimes you just don't have an hour to spare. If you simply don't have the time to read numerous books, then use the Look Inside feature that Amazon offers to read a snippet of the books. This can also give you a good idea of how other authors are approaching the topic you are writing about. However, I strongly encourage you to read the writing of your competition. How else will you be able to compete?

Again, the point of this exercise is to help set you up for success. These are some of the websites I visit when looking for additional ideas for my book.

1. Amazon
2. Google
3. Yahoo Answers
4. Twitter (Use the hashtag for your niche or genre)
5. Facebook Groups around your niche or genre
6. Blog, websites or forums around your niche or genre

It's not enough to just write a book anymore. Readers in your target audience are looking for good quality content. And you absolutely want to write good quality content so that your readers will leave you glowing reviews and tell others about your book. Nothing sells a book faster than word of mouth!

For fiction writers, your readers are looking for relatable yet meaningful characters, unpredictable plots, and strong dialogue. For non-fiction writers, your readers are looking for their problem to be solved, new ideas on old subject matters, and they really appreciate it when you over deliver. So begin your research and expand the original idea for your book!

Writer's Block And Tips For Avoiding It

Writer's block is something that will inevitably happen to most writers.

Because writing is such a creative process, there may be days when you're just not able to write. There are several reasons why this may happen. Maybe you just don't know how to advance your story, your creative juices aren't flowing on a particular day, or maybe you just have a lot of other things on your mind.

Over the span of my career, I've dealt with writer's block often, but through the years I've come up with a few ways to avoid the dreaded writer's block and keep it at bay.

Earlier in this chapter, I encouraged you to choose an idea for your book that you're passionate about. Not only will this help you to stay motivated to write, but it will also help you with avoiding writer's block. If you are writing on a topic that bores you, at some point you're going to be staring at a blank screen wondering, "What the hell do I write?" I'm sure you experienced this in high school or college when your teacher told you to write a 30-page paper on an absolutely boring topic and it was the most painful thing you'd ever experienced. Writing about something you are passionate about alleviates you not knowing where to start.

I would also encourage you to be knowledgeable about the topic you write on. This is especially true for non-fiction writers as your audience has an expectation that you are an expert or have extensive experience.

Writer's block can be avoided by writing about topics that excite you. For example, this book that you are currently reading excites me! I love sharing what I've learned with others and honestly, I have so many ideas for things I want to share, this book could go on forever. When you choose a topic that excites you, the likelihood of writer's block rearing its head will be slim to none.

Another effective way to keep writer's block at bay is to have a good idea of the direction you're going to take with your book. When I wrote my first book, I was very much a pantser. I had no clue what the characters in my book were going to do until they did it. And that worked fine for me until it didn't.

With subsequent books I've tried the concept of mind mapping, or what some call outlining. This is where you have a good idea of what each chapter is going to be about. You can even go so far as to outline the sub-chapters as well. I actually used mind mapping for this book that you're currently reading. As a result of me having laser focus, it took me only five days to complete the first draft of this book. Now how's that for getting the job done?

When you're outlining you don't have to be formal about it. Of course you can adopt the form of outlining that most of us learned in school. However it doesn't have to be that in depth. It can honestly be as simple as adding notes in your cellphone. Whether you choose to be a pantser or choose to do outlines is up to you. There is no right or wrong where this is concerned. This is all individualized and each writer should do what's comfortable for them.

However, if you start off as a pantser and you find that it absolutely doesn't work for you, don't be too proud to change your technique. I was very stubborn about being a pantser at first. I would proudly say that I could only write when I was inspired and that outlines felt too restrictive.

If I had the opportunity to go back and do it over, I would. I lost a lot of time with this mindset. While outlining does not ensure you won't deal with writer's block, it certainly helps to keep it in check.

So let's say you take all the necessary steps and you still deal with writer's block. Here are a few things I do if this happens:

1. If you're absolutely unable to write, go back and edit. Reread what you've already written. Change words that may not work. Elaborate on ideas. In doing so, you may trigger new ideas.

2. Make sure you're not distracted. If your phone is buzzing, social media distracts you, the television is on and your kids are calling for you, it will be difficult to concentrate. Try turning everything off and going to a quiet place.

3. Know your characters and know your plot. Sometimes writer's block can be caused by not knowing your characters or your plot prior to beginning your manuscript. Take time to get to know your characters and give thought to the purpose of your story. This doesn't mean that you have to have your entire story mapped out, but you do need a

general idea of what you are trying to achieve with your story and your characters. If you're writing with no direction, writer's block is likely to happen.

4. Go where the inspiration is. My novel *The Buzz* was largely based around the entertainment industry. So, I would visit entertainment websites and would sometimes go to nightclubs to draw inspiration for my book. Based on your story, where can you go to draw a little inspiration? Also, hang around people with personality traits similar to your characters. Look at   your time with them as time with your character.

5. Keep a notebook of ideas. As you're going about your day and thinking of ways to advance your story, write your ideas down. On a day when you have writer's block, those ideas will definitely come in handy. It may mean the difference between staring at white space and writing.

6. Let it go. If you are not on a deadline, then just walk away and come back when you have a little inspiration.

How To Make Time For Writing

Aspiring writers often wonder how they can make time to write? And rightfully so...

With all of the responsibilities we have as adults it does seem impossible to make time to write in an already busy day. However, I'm of the mindset – if you really want it, you'll make time for it!

Since I've been an adult, I've always had a busy schedule. Like you I've been busy doing what life demands of me like going to school, working, being a parent, and pursuing my dreams. There were days early on in my writing career where I came home from a stressful day at work, cooked dinner, spent time with my son, ran a blog, got ready for work the next day and then wrote for four hours. Weekends where I isolated myself in my room, because my characters were speaking to me and I couldn't let the inspiration pass. Mornings I went to work on two hours of sleep because the inspiration just wouldn't rest. There were days where I was downright tired of my manuscript because I'd read it THAT much.

Now of course I'm not recommending you go all renegade like I did (unless you want to), but there are easy ways that you can make time to write throughout your day without compromising any of your responsibilities. These are super simple tips that are going to make you go, "Wait what? No! I need something more scientific." I'm going to make this easy for you! You can implement these tips as soon as today.

Now I must warn you, you're going to have to make some sacrifices if you want to complete a manuscript. And you're going to make a lot of sacrifices, if you want your book to be good. I can't promise you that it will be easy, but I can promise you it's worth it!

Part of the reason we don't make time for writing is because we know that it is a huge undertaking. Completing your manuscript will require dedication, research, creativity, and last but not least, time (and a lot of it). So when time is an issue, how do we conquer it? Break it down into smaller segments!

Use whatever small window of opportunity you can grab until you can get your manuscript complete. If you have thirty minutes while your baby is down for a nap, take it! An hour while your son is at soccer, take it! A lunch break at work, take it! Take your computer with you and write on the train on your way to work. You'll be surprised at how much you can get accomplished.

Forget the idea that you don't have the time! Because you do! We all have the same twenty-four hours from which to work and there have been lots of people with lives just as busy as yours that has completed a manuscript. And damn it, you can too!

Okay, now that you know how to snatch time from everywhere you can get it, I'll share with you how to kick it up a notch so that you can knock multiple chapters out at a time. This will make the difference in you working on a manuscript for a really long time or a reasonable amount of time. For those of you who seek to be full-time writers, this is re-ally important for you.

The frequency and speed in which you write allows you to publish books faster. If it's taking you two years to write a book, you can imagine that your frequency will be a hindrance to your success. Really successful writers are publishing a few books per year. And I would also argue the longer it takes for you to write a book, the more likely you are to put it to the side.

If writing is your passion consider making sacrifices. I love TV like the next person, but I don't watch a lot of it. I'd rather use my TV time to advance my manuscript. Have you ever looked up and realized you'd just spent an hour on social media? Use that time to work on your manuscript instead!

I get it...we all need down time! But if you're rested why not use your down time to advance your manuscript? Make a habit of it and you'll find that you'll be more creative. You'll have loads of ideas to advance your story. You'll all of sudden find time that you never knew you had and before long you'll have a finished manuscript.

Now I've got to warn you! You're going to need to isolate yourself during your writing time. Choosing to make time for yourself just might make your friends and family uncomfortable. But remember, there's usually discomfort in the things we really want for ourselves. In time your friends and family will respect the fact that you need solitude in order to write.

If you usually sit with your buddies in the cafeteria for lunch, instead eat at a coffee shop and spend your lunch hour writing. Just think what you could get accomplished if you did this 5 days a week?

Some of you may be considering just taking time off from work to write. If you decide to take a sabbatical and write, use your time wisely! It's amazing how little time you think you have, and then when you get a bunch of time you flub it all away. You'll really need to be disciplined in order to get your manuscript completed because the time will go by quicker than you ever could imagine. But if you do have the luxury of being able to take time away from your full time job in order to write, it will greatly benefit you in the long run. Try your best to stick to a schedule and be just as stingy with your time as if you were working a job. Having stretches of time where you are able to write, will not only help you to get more written, but it will help you to become a better writer.

Now there are a few of you that I've still not managed to convince that you have time to write. And to you I ask, do you really want it? You do?

Take baby steps. Jot down plot twists, ideas for new characters, and ways to expand the story. When you do decide to make time to write, you'll have an idea of how to get started instead of staring at a blank page. As you start to see progress with your manuscript, it's easier to make it to the end.

Mind you, I'm speaking from experience! The closer I got to finishing my manuscript, the easier the writing became because I knew that I was so close to being done.

There are countless books providing tips on how to write a book in 30 days and in some cases even 7 days. For a newbie writer, I think it's important to focus on technique first over speed. As you get more experience, the writing will come easier and you will learn to crank out books at a faster speed naturally. It's also important as you are establishing yourself as an author, that you have quality content.

Rushing to put out a book will not be beneficial if the content can't compete with what's currently on the market. Once you know the blueprint for success, (which I'm providing for you in this book), this process will all be second nature to you. It's at that point that you will gain value from books that focus on learning to write expeditiously.

Lastly, if I could provide you with one piece of advice, it would be to stay committed to writing. I have quite a few clients who either begin working on their manuscript and then stop, or finish their manuscript and never take the next step. It has been my experience that when people step away from their manuscript for long periods of time, it's harder for them to regain the motivation they had when they initially started.

Every day you're away from your manuscript the likelihood of your completing it diminishes. Make the sacrifice today and make writing a priority! In six months, you'll have most of your free time back and can proudly proclaim that you're a published author!

Now that I've provided you with a few suggestions on where to get ideas from and how to make time for writing, the next step is getting your manuscript onto your computer.

Honestly when it comes to software, I have to admit that I'm pretty old school. I have been using Microsoft Word since the beginning of time. It's what I'm comfortable using and honestly, I will probably stick to it.

However, I've heard from my clients that Google Docs and the software program Scrivener are good alternatives as well. Whatever you decide, choose software that doesn't have a steep learning curve and that you can jump into rather quickly. This is important because the longer you have to fiddle around with software, the more likely you are not to write.

Formatting Your Manuscript

Formatting your manuscript correctly from the start is important for a number of reasons. At some point you are going to pass your manuscript off to someone to provide a manuscript critique, or to a beta reader, an editor or even a reviewer. Because of this, the publishing industry has adopted a general set of guidelines with respects to formatting a manuscript. Now of course, you can format it in whatever way you want and then change it when you need to share your document. However, I recommend doing it right from the start to make it easier.

Here are the basic guidelines for formatting a manuscript:

- 1″ margins
- 12 pt font
- Times New Roman, Arial, or Courier font
- Double spaced
- Title page (includes physical & email address, title, and word count)
- Header (includes name and title of manuscript on the left and page number on the right)

It's also important to note that you should always check the website of the company you're submitting to and view their guidelines before procceding with the above. In some cases, publishers, agents, and editors might have their own set of submission guidelines. In the event that there are none, it's advised that you use the aforementioned formatting.

Understanding Word Count

As you begin writing, at some point you're going to wonder exactly how long your book should be?

There are a few things you need to consider with respect to word count (or book length). First, are you writing an eBook or a print book? Is your book fiction or non-fiction? What genre are you writing?

eBooks have really changed the game with respect to word count. Short has truly become the new long. Many of the most popular eBooks are short by most standards and don't at all rival the word count of their print counterparts. This is beneficial for writers for a number of reasons. First, it allows you to break down bigger ideas into a series of books.

For instance, instead of going into great detail about marketing in this book, which would be overwhelming for an aspiring writer, I will instead follow this book with a book that focuses solely on book marketing. Speaking of which, stay tuned until the end where I offer that book as a bonus!

Secondly, the cost to publish an eBook is significantly lower in comparison to publishing a print book. So one of the biggest advantages of writing an eBook is that you can test your market, and if they respond well, you can follow up with a print version of your book.

We live in a microwave society. Our readers want their information quick quick quick! No longer are readers willing to read through a hundred pages of fluff to get to the meat and potatoes of the book. And quite frankly this should entice you to write, knowing that you can really get to the heart of your story and move on to your next manuscript.

Avid readers have the potential to have access to hundreds of books on their readers and smartphone reading apps. People are reading in airports, coffee shops and even on their lunch breaks. How valuable would it be for you, the author, to provide them well-written books that they could take advantage of during these short periods of time?

Not to mention that readers now have the ability to instantly download your book. Long gone are the days where you physically have to leave your house to purchase a book. Gone are the days where you have to spend $12.99 on a book that might take you a month to read.

Authors are now even offering some of their eBooks for free. When was the last time you walked into a bookstore and they gave you a free book or even a book for $2.99? With eBooks starting at such a low price point (either free or $0.99), buyers are more apt to give your book a try. Even if a reader doesn't own a Kindle, as long as they have a tablet or a smartphone, they can just download the app and begin reading your book in minutes.

eBooks typically need to start at a word count of 10,000 words in order to truly be valuable. This is also important because if your book is published through Amazon Kindle, the Look Inside feature shows the opening of your book. If your book falls under 10,000 words the likelihood of the most important parts of your book being shown is greater. After all who needs to read a book when they've seen it all in the preview?

If you do decide to write a shorter eBook, please consider what we discussed about value. Quality content is even more important with an eBook. Readers are not giving any leeway to writers just because they decided to write a shorter book. They are still expecting value for their money and time.

If you decide that you still want to write a longer book then by all means write it! Some content just requires a larger word count. Don't let the fact that short is the new long discourage you from writing and fleshing out all of your ideas.

As far as print books are concerned, writers should follow the word count guidelines established by the publishing industry. One of the reasons this is important is because of the actual printing of the book. If your book is too small, the printer will be unable to create a spine for your book. Also, with respects to print books, the expectation has been set for a more thorough and well-researched book.

With that being said, there are some situations where a print book just makes good sense. For instance, if you are a non-fiction writer who has clients or who does speaking engagements, having your book prominently displayed on a table will be a great way for you to sell directly to your target audience. Perhaps you are a personal fitness trainer; a book would be great to pitch to your client. It will arm them with a lot of your expertise and experience all at once.

Print books are also useful for book signings. While I've certainly seen people do book signings for eBooks, there are some readers who prefer that authors sign a copy of their physical book.

Whether you are writing fiction or non-fiction consider the fact that there are some genres that allow for a bigger word count. For instance, the sci-fi and fantasy genres typically have larger word counts. For that reason, I encourage each of you to type your genre along with the words "word count" into Google and see what the industry standard is. This will give you an idea of how many words to write.

CHAPTER TWO

CATERING TO YOUR TARGET AUDIENCE

Quite often when I do a consultation with a new writer, they'll explain to me how their book is for everyone. While there are some books that can benefit a large audience, I can't think of any books that are for everyone. If this is your current mindset, I would encourage you to rethink target audiences.

Understanding target audiences will be vital to how you write and the success of your book. In an earlier chapter, we talked briefly about identifying your target audience and discovering their age, what websites they visit, the groups they belong to on social media, their worries, their concerns, and their likes. These are the initial steps you would take in discovering the perfect reader for your book.

Now we're going to discuss why you need to know all of this and how by knowing this you are better positioning your book to resonate with the intended readers.

In general, the books I write are for writers. But when I really begin to think about the ideal person to read my book, that person would be an aspiring writer. So from that huge pool of writers, my niche just became smaller.

While there will be some more advanced writers who may benefit from one or two of the tips I share, the person who will benefit the most from my book would be: a person who's never written a book, a person who seeks answers to their many writing and publishing related questions, or a new writer that wants to know the blueprint for success right from the beginning.

Think about it like this…if I were to dump every writer in the world into a funnel, the ones who fall through at the bottom would be my target audience.

If a writer were to type "writing" or some related search term into the search box on Amazon, I would attract a pool of writers (both aspiring and established). However, as these writers further explore my title and book description I will either engage them or they'll realize that my book isn't for them.

However, there will be those aspiring writers who'll say, "Yes, this is exactly what I'm looking for!" And it's these people who I'll sell and deliver to. These are the people who are a part of my target audience.

This concept is very much the same for fiction writers. My first book, *The Buzz: When Celebrity Gossip Goes Wrong* centers around the entertainment world, specifically hip-hop culture. So I can assume that my demographic would be men and women who appreciate hip-hop and pop culture. These would be the people visiting websites like TMZ and other gossip blogs. These are also avid readers of urban fiction books.

So when I write, I have to write in a way that resonates with this reader. If my book reads like a Shakespearean play, do you think my audience will leave me a good review?

Knowing the likes, needs, and expectations of the demographic you write for, allows you to write specifically for that audience. It helps you to cater to your reader's expectation.

Please don't mistake this for losing your voice!

Instead, it ensures that you are attracting the people that should be reading your book and weeds out the people who won't find value. Now of course there will be one or two that will slip through the cracks, but for the most part your audience will find you. How do I know? Because you are reading this book!

Understanding your audience will help you to write content that suits them, craft an engaging title that attracts them, and to write a compelling book description that delivers!

While writing your manuscript, write for the one person that will benefit from your book the most. And in doing so, you'll attract the people who'll leave you positive reviews, share your books with friends and family, follow you on all of your social media, and support your writing career every step of the way!

Who is your target audience? And how can you cater to them?

CHAPTER THREE

SELF-PUBLISHING VS. TRADITIONAL PUBLISHING

One of the most important decisions you'll make with respects to your writing career is how you will publish your manuscript. In this chapter, we will discuss the differences between self-publishing and traditional publishing so that you'll be in a position to make an informed decision on the publishing method you choose.

The main things you'll need to consider are your goals as an author, your skillset, your budget, and how much time you want to invest in the process. It would also be wise to give thought to how you want your final book to be published. For instance, do you want your book to be a print book or an eBook? I'll explain why this should be a part of your decision later.

First, let's start with traditional publishing since this is where the industry started.

Signing to a traditional publishing house definitely has its upsides. First and foremost, it establishes credibility with your audience. Consider the music industry for a moment. When you hear that an artist has been signed to Sony Records, as a buyer, our tendency is to trust the music a little more. The assumption is that there was a gatekeeper that listened to this artist's music and co-signed that the music was in fact good. Now of course this is all subjective, but you get the point.

The same holds true with being signed to a publishing company. Being signed to Harper Collins gives legitimacy to an author's writing.

With that being said, competition is steep within the traditional publishing world because publishers are looking for the best of the best.

To make it even more challenging, prior to signing to a publishing company you first have to grab the attention of a literary agent. Be mindful that you should only be querying agents that are actually accepting the genre you write. In other words, sending your romance manuscript to a children's book agent will not do you much good.

There are several ways to find a literary agent. A common and the most suggested way is to look at the acknowledgments in an author's book. Of course the author should write in the same genre as you.

Another great way to find an agent, and one I recommend, is for writers to visit http://agentquery.com. This website serves as a database of literary agents. This free service allows you to narrow your agent search by keyword, genre, and whether the agent is actively seeking new clients.

Because your literary agent will work on your behalf, you will rightfully pay them a commission when they sell your book. In other words, you should not be paying an agent if they haven't sold your book! Your literary agent will make suggestions on ways you can improve your manuscript, submit your manuscript to publishing houses they think will fit your manuscript best, and work with your best interest at heart. This is a decision not to be taken lightly. You want to choose a literary agent that believes in you, one who's responsive and most importantly one that has contacts within the publishing industry.

Signing to a traditional publishing company ensures you have a team of people who are working to publish the best version of your book. This team will help you to handle copyrights, secure ISBNs, handle accounting, develop a marketing plan, get your book into book stores, set up a media tour, and most importantly, they will fund the printing and publishing of your book. Because they assume the financial risk, they will pay you a royalty. Also if they think you are worth it they may even offer you a small advance. (Larger advances are usually reserved for more established authors).

A traditional publisher has extensive publishing experience. As such they will be able to make recommendations with respects to titles, covers, editing of the book, and anything from characters to plot development.

With a traditional publisher you will share creative control. What this means is, you might have an idea for a book cover or a really catchy idea for a title. If the publishing company you're signed to doesn't agree, they will likely trump you and make the final decision.

Signing to a traditional publishing company does not ensure your success. In fact it can be quite the waiting game, sometimes taking writers between one and two years before they are able to secure a publishing house, if ever. Once signed, it's still the author's responsibility to market their book and while the publishing company will assist on some level, the bulk of the responsibility falls in the author's lap.

Because they are footing the bill so to speak, the publishing company will need to be repaid. So it may be a while before you see any profits because you'll need to repay any advances or upfront expenses.

Lastly, being signed to a traditional publishing company means you will be bound by contractual deadlines. In other words if they say your book is due on January 1st, you can't counter with, "But I have writer's block!" And if your book doesn't do well, it may keep you from landing another deal.

With that being said, the traditional publishing model is tried and true. If you don't want the responsibility of having to put all the pieces of the puzzle together, this may be a better route for you.

Lastly, be wary of these companies that ask you to submit a manuscript and then lead you to believe they've picked your manuscript out of the thousands they've received. After that, they'll then tell you to submit a payment of $5,000 to publish your book.

That is not being traditionally signed! That is self-publishing! And it's important that you know the difference. There are so many new authors that are naïve to this bait and switch routine, that many are being duped into buying expensive publishing packages under the pretense that they've been "selected." And let me be clear this is not the writer's fault! These companies are clearly taking advantage of people who are eager to be signed. When in doubt, remember this rule:

If a company asks you for money, you are NOT being traditionally published!

When I started writing my first book, it was my intention to traditionally publish. This was about ten years ago and self-publishing wasn't as prevalent as it is now. When I think back on my mindset, all I can do is giggle because I really thought that self-publishing consisted of solely selling books in Walmart parking lots. Am I the only person who thought this?

Oh, I am? Don't judge me.

While I definitely consider myself to be persuasive, I am not a salesman! So self-publishing was initially a no go!

Once my manuscript was completed, I sent query letters off to a few agents. However, as I started to do research I realized that my writing goals were more in line with that of self-publishing. And because my book was time-sensitive, if I chose to go the traditional publishing route, I would need to find an agent and, in turn, a publishing company quickly or else I would be forced to do extensive rewrites.

The main reason I decided that self-publishing made more sense for me is the creative control aspect. If you knew me personally, you would understand why this was important. I am quite the creative person and even during the writing process, I had the entire project mapped out in my mind. I had the book title all picked out, I knew exactly how I wanted the cover to look, and quite frankly, I was pleased with the final draft of my manuscript and didn't want anyone telling me to change significant parts of my story. As a creative person at heart, every aspect of publishing excited me. I was more than eager to put all of the pieces together to create a final product.

Aside from that, I'd also seen a few success stories that made me think, "Hmm...I can definitely do this!" The one that stands out the most was an interview I saw one day while off from work. Even to this day I feel that I was meant to be home to see that author being interviewed.

On the talk show the self-published author shared how she'd sold tens of thousands of copies of her book. How you may ask? Well this was back before writers knew how to really use the Internet for marketing, so she'd hand sold copies of her book to booksellers and book readers in and around Philadelphia. It was something about her determination that sparked something in me. It made me go, "Well perhaps I can do this too!"

The fact that there was now social media to help me market my book, and the fact that I understood publicity through my time freelancing, were all indications that I might want to give this self-publishing thing a try.

So I assembled my own team of a photographer, book cover designer, and an editor. Luckily I had some experience in web design so I built my own sites and I purchased a software program that allowed me to typeset my books. It was extremely important that my book look as good as any traditionally published book, so I spent a great deal of time and effort seeking out professionals who could help me achieve the finished product I desired.

In the self-publishing world there are no gatekeepers. Essentially, you can finish your manuscript today and if you wanted to publish an eBook for example, you can have it up on Amazon Kindle tomorrow. It's because of that there's great scrutiny that follows self-publishing. Readers are usually more critical of how self-published books look as well as the editing or lack thereof. It's for this reason that I advise my clients to be mindful of their responsibility as a writer if they choose to self-publish. After all, this is your brand and your book is the first representation of you.

While you won't necessarily have a ready-made team supporting you as in the traditional publishing world, you will have the freedom to assemble your own team. And while it took a bit of footwork initially, I thoroughly enjoyed the process and my final product.

As with traditional publishing there are pros to self-publishing as well. If rejection is one of your concerns, there's no need to send out query letters and receive letters of rejection. Instead, you publish whatever you want, whenever you want.

As I described earlier, you have full creative control over everything. And I would advise you to take that responsibility seriously. Again, look at your competition, how does their finished product look? Can yours compete? Did you get a manuscript critique for suggestions on improvement? Did you give your final draft to a group of beta readers to see how your target audience will respond? Is your book properly edited? Did you choose an engaging title that includes keywords your target audience would be searching for? Is your book cover professional? Is your book description engaging and does it have a call-to-action? Did you do research in advance of writing your manuscript to determine if you are writing in a profitable niche? Did you price your book competitively?

Because you are footing all the costs, any profits you make are yours! There's no waiting for a publisher to recoup costs and for them to pay you royalties, all monies will come directly to you. With that being said, I encourage self-published authors to really give thought to self-publishing costs.

It's kind of like when you are a first time parent, and you run out and buy every gadget, toy, and clothing item hoping that you'll use it all. Only to discover that it wasn't as essential as you thought it would be. Well, self-publishing can kind of be the same thing, especially for those writers who decide to publish physical copies of their books. Buying the most expensive publishing package and a thousand bookmarks and hundreds of books that sit in your garage are all expenses that you have control over.

I've compiled a list of all the costs a self-published author can incur and I encourage you to view it at the attached link http://thewriteoneblog.com/self-publishing-costs/.

Obviously there are some things you won't have a choice in purchasing like ISBNs and copyright protection. However, shop around for printing and editing and see where you can get the best deals. With respect to where you should put the most attention, I would say that should be in editing. By far, editing is the most important part of the publishing process and it's a step that should never be skipped.

Keep a record of every dime you spend. This will help you in determining your break-even cost. In other words, you'll need to determine how many books you'll need to sell in order to recoup the money you spent. Any monies you make above this amount can be considered to be profit! Set a budget and try your best to stick to it! However, be reasonable in determining how much services cost. For example, editing can be quite expensive depending on the person you choose.

While I have personally only had experience with two companies for the printing of my books, http://lightningsource.com and http://createspace.com (and by the way I'm extremely pleased with the quality they provide),

I will make mention of a few other companies based on my client's recommendations.

1. http://ingramspark.com
2. http://bookbaby.com
3. http://lulu.com
4. http://smashwords.com

No matter the company you choose, remember that you're the overseer of the quality! Ask for samples (where possible), do research online, read other people's experiences, and make sure the company you choose is responsive! Is it important for you to be able to get someone on the phone as opposed to email support? Does their final product rival that of a traditional publishing company? Do they accept returns of your printed books so that you're able to get your book in bookstores? Do they have other distribution channels available such as retail stores, libraries and other book retailers besides Amazon? All of these factors should be considered before committing to a publishing platform.

Now earlier I said you should give thought to how you want your final product to look. If you make the decision that you want your final product to be an eBook only, there are so many cost effective ways to make this happen. The most money you'll spend in this regard would be on editing.

Otherwise, everything else can be done on a budget by utilizing websites like http://fiverr.com, http://upwork.com or http://bookdesigntemplates.com.

If you just want to stick your toe in the water, eBooks are a great way to do so. This allows you to test out your market and get a good understanding of the type of income you'll be able to make. It's because of this that some authors who don't necessarily have an interest in print copies of their book, choose to self-publish their own eBooks instead of going the traditional publishing route.

Another successful model that writers are following is the hybrid model. This model allows a writer to start off with one publishing method and then move on to the next.

For example, traditional publishing companies are a lot more selective in the authors they are choosing now. They are looking for different attributes in addition to being a great writer. They are looking at the number of books you've sold on your own, social media followings and engagement on author blogs.

As a result, some authors are choosing to build their fan base as a self-published author first and then approach or in some cases be found by traditional publishing companies. The leverage this model provides is awesome with respects to advances, negotiating royalties, and keeping a bit of creative control.

This model can also happen in the reverse, where traditionally published authors choose to try their hand at self-publishing since they already have an established fan base and have sold a number of books.

There's no right or wrong with respects to your decision to self-publish or traditionally publish and choosing to go one route and then later deciding to do something else are all options. Assess what your overall goals are as writer. Be honest about the time commitment and the financial investment you want to make and work to make that happen!

CHAPTER FOUR

THE BLUEPRINT FOR SUCCESS

The information I've shared thus far is all essential to being a success in the publishing industry. Books become bestsellers because they are well written and there's a market for them. Writers are successful because they've written enough quality books to establish a career.

I encourage you to take the information you've learned while reading *How To Write Your First Book* and exceed any goals that you've set for yourself. The opportunities are endless for writers who know the blueprint for success, are passionate, and great at marketing books.

The W.R.I.T.E. Formula

To recap, the blueprint for success is all in an acronym I've created called the W.R.I.T.E. formula.

Write
Research

be Imaginative

Thorough and

Engaging

If you follow this tried and true formula, you will find great success in your writing career. Let's go over the blueprint for success one last time. If you follow this to a tee, you're ready to move on to the next component of marketing your book.

Write. The only way to be a successful writer is to write. Make a commitment to write at least five days a week. The best writing tip I can give you is to start your book with a strong opening no matter the genre you write!

If you write non-fiction, answer your reader's questions, solve their problems and motivate them. If you write fiction, create memorable characters and make them flawed.

Using this formula will be beneficial in readers maintaining interest in your book, and a strong introduction will also help you to further sell your book.

As I mentioned earlier, Amazon allows readers to view the first pages of your book and, quite often, readers use this to gauge whether or not they will take the next step and click the button to buy. So start strong, keep the pace, and end strong!

Remember when you initially start writing your manuscript you are just working on a first draft. I doubt there's a writer alive who actually publishes a first draft of anything they've written. Gosh, I would be so scared to!

Don't put a lot of pressure on yourself. Your first draft doesn't have to be perfect; you just need a starting point. Once you've completed your first draft, give your manuscript to a writing coach like myself for a manuscript critique, so that they can provide suggestions for improvements.

Once you've completed your second draft, give your manuscript to a group of beta readers so they can provide you with an additional set of improvements. These are people in your target audience who are avid readers of the genre you write. By the time you have a professional and your target audience to review your manuscript, you will have the best final draft possible.

If you're anything like me, perfection may be something you struggle with. With my first four books, I had a really difficult time releasing the books into the world. These were my babies and I wanted them to be perfect! So I would read, re-read, and read it again, hoping that I could make it better than it already was.

While I still somewhat have this trait, I've learned to let it go! The more you write, the better you'll become.

Research. Aside from quality writing this is probably one of the most important steps you can take in ensuring that your book will be a success. While it may seem like a lot of extra work, research will save you time, money, and frustration knowing that you are writing a book in a genre that is marketable and will sell. With so many books on the market, it's important to spend the time researching your competition, reading their work, and setting yourself apart.

Let's be clear - your research shouldn't stop at what your competition is writing! You should also be researching book covers, book descriptions, titles, and pricing.

Pricing is one of those components that have killed many a self-published book. Think about it like this, if you price your book higher than the next guy, you are pricing yourself right out of the competition. I've seen this happen time and time again. Self-published authors, who are trying to recoup their upfront expenses, do so on the backs of the consumers not knowing that they are instead sinking their books before they ever get a chance. Every single thing you do should be competitive from the writing to the pricing!

Be *Imaginative.* Writing is creative, so use your imagination to bring your book idea to life. There's probably not a book idea that you can think of that hasn't already been written.

So what makes your book special? You!

You have a unique perspective that no one else can provide. Use that to your advantage whether you are writing fiction or non-fiction. Tell your story in the unique way only you can deliver, stay true to your voice, and know that there are people eager to read it!

Be *Thorough.* This is something I share with my clients, especially those interested in writing shorter books.

Just because a book is short on pages, doesn't mean it has to be short on information. Unless intentional, don't leave any unanswered questions. Develop your characters and your plot thoroughly and if you are covering a topic in your non-fiction book make sure you dot every I and cross every T.

Be *Engaging.* While writing is certainly an important aspect, a book can't be successful without engaging your audience. I go into this in detail in my book *How To Market Your First Book.* However, in short, effective book marketing is essential to retaining readers. And just so you know, book marketing should start while you're writing your book and not once it's been completed. Use social media, your blog and/or website, your Amazon Author Central page, and whatever avenues you can think of to engage your target audience. Experts say - all you need is a thousand core fans and with that, you have the springboard for a successful career.

In conclusion, I would be doing you a disservice if I didn't tell you that there might be pitfalls and roadblocks that you encounter along the way. Don't let them deter you! Pitfalls are there to separate the strong from the weak. To determine who wants it bad enough and who's willing to give up.

Over the span of my writing career there were times where I thought, "Maybe it's true...maybe writing is just what you should be doing as a hobby."

Writing has forced me to work harder than I ever have in my entire life and the rewards have not always matched my effort. If not for faith, I would have given up a million times. However, when you know your purpose it's hard to accept defeat.

I remember asking myself, "Why would writing be my strongest talent if I weren't supposed to do something with it?"

Writing has brought me so much joy dating as far back as my childhood. Even though I didn't know how to verbalize it as a little girl, I knew that using my words was what I was meant to do.

The nature of writing requires you to invest a lot in the beginning, without compensation. But isn't that true for most things? You go to college for four years before you get a career.

So be mindful of this and as I said before, give yourself an opportunity for your dreams to manifest. You'll spend time doing the research, you'll spend time creating the idea, you'll spend time writing the book, you'll spend time publishing the book, and then you'll spend time marketing. But the feeling you get when you hold your book in your hands for the first time is indescribable.

And I can't even begin to tell you how it feels when others acknowledge your work through reviews and write-ups.

I remember one of the very first emails I received from a reader. He wrote me and told me he had stayed up all night reading my book *The Buzz*. He told me it was so good he couldn't put it down. I was like, "What?!? My book? Are you serious?"

Or what about the text I received from a friend that read, "I'm finished! 5 stars…bravo my friend ;)"

There are scores of people who have taken their talent, expertise, and experience and created a career for themselves. I am one such person.

I married all of my talents and created a business where I help people to do what I love – write. And as a bonus I get to create awesome books too!

This book has provided you with a head start in your writing career. However, none of what you've learned will work if you don't apply it. There are countless people who go to 'how to be a success' workshops and seminars every year, but it's only a small percentage of people that actually apply the information they've learned.

The same goes for 'how to be a success' books. What benefit will you gain from this book if you don't apply the information shared?

So guess what? I'm holding you accountable! Jot down the idea that you're most passionate about and begin the research. Once you've gotten your idea, I want you to contact me at 1-877-85-WRITE (859-7483) and I will provide you with a FREE 30 minute strategy session where I will help you to develop your book idea.

I sincerely hope you've found value in this book! This book was truly a labor of love and something I wanted to share with aspiring writers to encourage them to give writing a try!

If you're so inclined, I'd love a review on Amazon of *How To Write Your First Book*. Reviews are a huge help to authors. As a thank you, please find on the subsequent pages a bonus book – *How To Market Your First Book*!

CHAPTER FIVE

HOW TO MARKET YOUR FIRST BOOK

Congratulations! If you're reading this then you are either writing, recently completed, or have already released your first book. As I'm sure you know from dedicating time and creativity to your manuscript; writing is a very fulfilling and cathartic process, an accomplishment that should be commended.

How To Market Your First Book is meant to assist you on your writing journey. It doesn't matter if you've completed your manuscript or if your book is only an idea. It also doesn't matter whether you decide to self-publish or be traditionally published.

This is the barebones approach to developing and executing a strategic marketing plan to increase your presence and drive sales.

This book differs from others on the market because it takes into consideration that you are marketing your first book. And it's because of that distinction you need to strategize differently than authors who are already established.

As an author with no fan base or a smaller fan base there are certain steps that you need to take first, to ensure that you are setting your book up for success. I have taken all of this into consideration and will provide you with tips on how to navigate marketing for your first book, establishing a readership, and how to make your book stand out from the crowd.

This book will focus on traditional marketing approaches for writers, but also touch on social networking sites.

It will provide tactics for getting publicity to help build brand awareness for you and your book.

So sit back and get ready to take your writing career to the next level! You deserve it!

CHAPTER SIX

YOUR VERY FIRST BOOK LAUNCH

If I'd written this book even just a year ago, I would have shared drastically different advice than what I'm going to share in this chapter. As someone who's been published for several years now, my viewpoint has changed considerably as it relates to book marketing. And as a disclaimer, your views will change too! As you learn more and gain more experience, everything by way of book marketing is up for reconsideration.

Depending on the book marketing resources you find in your research, I've discovered that some tips will be very basic while others can put you in a position to have a very profitable career. So I encourage all of you reading this book to never stop seeking out information on book marketing or publishing in general. Sometimes it takes just one small tweak to an already existing marketing plan to take you from selling a few copies per month, to a considerable amount.

A few years ago, I would have told you to market your book in as many places as you can to gain maximum exposure for your book. While I still consider that kind of marketing to be beneficial, I now believe that to be a bonus and something you should do in conjunction with the steps I'm going to propose in this chapter.

When I published my first book, I thought book marketing consisted of merely letting people know about your book via book signings, social media, publicity, etc.

Keep in mind; I published my first book in 2008. Self-publishing was just gaining some traction and there weren't as many resources then as there are now. In all of my research (and I did a lot of it), none of the resources I found shared the importance of setting your book up correctly on Amazon, essentially allowing Amazon to help market your book.

Amazon is one of the biggest book retailers and they house the credit cards of millions of their customers who are eager to purchase everything from books to clothing. Think about that for a second. The fact that customers even allow Amazon to save their credit cards speaks volumes about the trust Amazon has gained.

Amazon successfully caters to their customers and ensures a very tailored customer experience by providing relevant results. They even go so far as to suggest the next books customers should read based off previous buying patterns. Just think what this means for us as writers. Essentially this means that if we have all the right elements: a great title, book cover, book description, our books placed in the right categories, and the correct keywords attached, Amazon will help us to market our book. This is huge!

As a book coach I have talked to so many writers that have absolutely no interest in doing extensive marketing of their books. That is not to say that setting up your book on Amazon relieves you of book marketing, but if done correctly, it certainly lightens your load.

Back when I was a newly published author I had no idea that there was a strategy to putting your book on Amazon. As a result, my book sold well initially. It also sold well through book promotions and when I was actively marketing it. However, once my book had been published for a while and I was no longer putting the same time and effort into book marketing as I had been, my book sales started to wane. For a long time, I thought that was just normal for an older book. That is until I realized that other writers were still gaining traction with their older catalogue of books because Amazon was essentially doing the marketing for them.

To put this in perspective, there is going to be a period of time when we as authors are actively marketing our books. But then after three to six months or maybe even a year, we aren't going to be marketing our books with the same fervor we had when the book was first released. So what will that mean for sales?

As a newbie author, your challenges are going to be different than that of an established author. An established author already has a fan base of readers actively seeking out their books, whereas a newly published author is having to find their audience one reader at a time.

In traditional book marketing we find these readers by seeking out book clubs, finding avid readers on sites like GoodReads, doing blog hops, book signings, marketing on social media, and the like. While all of these are extremely useful and necessary in getting your name out, what happens when you're tired? Or when you want to begin writing your next book? Or when you've flooded the fan base you do have? What can you do to market your book that will help you sell copies while you sleep?

What I'm about to share was a huge "aha" moment for me. Now remember, your best chance for exposure is when your book is first released. While Amazon is a bit mum on the algorithm for showing books to potential customers, we do know that they take into consideration: sales history, how long your book has been published, keywords, categories, clicks, title, and ranking.

If this step is done correctly, then book signings, social media, and all other book marketing tactics we'll discuss later, will act as a bonus to the boost in exposure Amazon will provide.

Much of what I will share in this chapter will be focused on Amazon. For one, it's the book retailer I know the best and two, a good percentage of your books will be sold through their site. While I think it's important to know how to successfully market on all of the book retailer sites, this book is written with the newbie writer in mind. And it's for that reason that I encourage you to master one retailer at a time, and then take what you've learned and apply it to the next retailer and tweak your strategy as you see fit.

If you read the first book in this series *How To Write Your First Book*, you know that I put a lot of emphasis on doing research on whether the topic you are writing is marketable. If you skip this step, much of what will be offered in this chapter and/or book will be useless.

It's impossible for your marketing to be effective if you don't have anyone to market to, so before you write a single word I encourage you to put your pen down and go do research and see if you're actually writing in a marketable niche.

However, for the sake of bringing you up to speed, the point of doing this research is to estimate how much money can be made on the topic you're writing about. For instance, what if you have a really good book idea but there's no market for it, or no proven sales, would you still write the book? In most cases, I'm sure the answer would be no. So determining the profitability of your genre/or niche alleviates you writing a book that has no market.

Although this step needs to be done prior to writing your book, I'll discuss this topic briefly.

The first step in determining profitability would be to find the potential categories you'd want to place your book in. Once you've determined this you would then look at the rankings of the books in these categories to determine how well the books are selling.

Once you've clicked into a category, Amazon will show 16 results. You will need to check the ranking of each of these 16 books to see if this category is profitable. You can find a book's ranking by clicking on each book and scrolling down to the Product Details section. Once there, you should find what's called the Amazon Best Sellers Rank. If the rankings for the first 16 book results are anywhere from 1 to 100,000, it's safe to say that it's a profitable category. To put this in perspective, there are over eight million books on Amazon. If a book is ranked between 1 and 100,000 that means the book is selling pretty well on a daily basis.

Once you've found potential categories that work for your book, you'll need to choose two. My recommendation is to find as many categories as possible that will work for your book. In the event that one doesn't work well, or stops working for you in the future, you'll have additional categories to choose from.

With respect to categories, choose categories that relate to your book, but remember all categories won't be a perfect fit. If you are having a difficult time finding the perfect category, search for books on Amazon that relates to your book's subject matter. Once you've found a book, click on the book's page and scroll down to the section called Amazon Best Sellers Rank. There you should find some category ideas. And lastly, if you scroll all the way to the bottom of the page, you should see a section called Look for Similar Items by Category, where you will get additional ideas for categories.

Amazon allows you to place your book into two categories. However, I strongly advise you to choose two categories that have different paths. You want to choose two different paths because doing so gives your book more exposure.

So let's say your book is a cookbook. Your first category path may start: Books > Health, Fitness & Dieting >.

However only choose one category that begins this way. Your second path could begin Books > Cookbooks, Food & Wine > Special Diet > as this gives you exposure to two additional audiences.

Choosing the two above-mentioned categories would mean your book is being shown in:

Books
Health, Fitness & Dieting
Cookbooks, Food & Wine
Special Diet

Whereas, let's say you chose two identical paths in the Health, Fitness & Dieting category, your book would only be shown in:

Books
Health, Fitness & Dieting

As I said before, every category won't be the perfect fit. This is merely because every reader will search differently. And to be clear, the same goes for keywords!

Keywords are the words or string of words that buyers will be putting into Amazon when they are searching for a book on a particular subject. Compile a list of all the keywords that are associated with your book. Include keywords that relate to genre, setting, character types, character roles, plot themes, and story tone. For non-fiction, choose keywords that relate to the topic you are writing about.

Keywords are going to be used for several things throughout this process, including: research to determine profitability, crafting your book title, and lastly, they will be used in the back end of Amazon once you upload your book. So make sure you compile a solid list!

Once you have your list, put these keywords into Amazon's search bar one at a time and select whether you are searching the Kindle Store or Books. This selection will be dependent on how you choose to publish your book. For example, if you are going to publish strictly on Kindle, choose the Kindle Store. If you are going to do a print version of your book, select the Books option. Also, if you are publishing both an eBook and a print version of your book, Amazon considers this to be two books.

Amazon will link the books to each other, however it'll be shown in the appropriate section - either Kindle or Books, depending on the version. This will obviously provide your book additional exposure!

Once you've placed your keyword in the search box and the results show up, check the books and first determine whether the books are similar to your book. If they are, then as with categories, check that the rankings are within 100,000. You would do this for all of your keywords, until you have a profitable bunch.

As a tip, use Google's keyword tool for additional keyword suggestions, and also ask friends and family what keywords come to mind when they think of your book.

Because we all search differently, only using our own suggestions limits us, but if we ask others and use the Google Keyword Suggestion tool, we can find even better keywords that may be more profitable than the keywords we choose. Once you've found your keywords, these are also going to be the keywords you supply to Amazon prior to uploading. If you choose to publish both an eBook and print book, then your categories and keywords should mirror on both the Book side as well as in the Kindle Store.

Be mindful that this research will take a considerable amount of time. Depending on the book's subject matter, it's taken me upwards of seven or eight hours in some cases to do the research. However if you put the time in now, you will reap the benefits later.

If this all sounds like too much, I offer a video course that shows exactly how to do this step as well as walks you through the entire first year of publishing. For more information on the How To Write A Book video course, visit my website. Or if you want more information on how to strategize with keywords and categories, I strongly recommend *Let's Get Visible* by David Gaughran. His book is dedicated to Amazon SEO and he shares a lot of great tips.

If you find that both your categories and keywords are profitable, then the first step in this book marketing process is crafting a title.

How Book Titles Help Market Your Book

Book titles are important! Your title is the first indication to Amazon and readers as to what your book is about. Amazon uses the keywords within your book title to provide relevant results to their customers.

While creativity is important with a book title, it's equally important that you use keywords that your target audience is searching for. Great book titles will help your book gain a lot of exposure and, in turn, help you to sell more books.

Before I go into more detail about how important keywords are with respects to your title, I want to share how one of my earlier books was hindered by its title. As a matter of fact, two of my earlier books were affected by not crafting a title that included keywords.

While my co-author and I were writing the book we came up with the title, Pull Your Pants Up and be a man! We thought it was the perfect title and by all accounts it was. It was catchy, it evoked conversation and thought, but what it didn't do was speak to what the book was about. Although the book was geared towards minority boys between the ages of 13 and 18 and was a self-empowerment book, based on the title our audience thought the book was condemning the youth and their fashion choices.

At the time we were so new to publishing we had no idea the importance of including keywords in the title to convey exactly what the book was about. Honestly I'd seen enough catchy book titles that I thought it was a perfect title. And it is… if you're an already established author with a huge fan base. But for a new writer who has no one necessarily searching for their books, you need as big of a head start as you can get. Book titles are one such head start.

When my co-author and I published to Amazon we would get a few sales here or there, but it didn't catch on like we thought it would. Especially when we tired of book marketing.

Once I started to do research on how to get more exposure on Amazon, I realized the reason it wasn't gaining any traction was because I hadn't included any keywords in the title or subtitle (which is extremely important for non-fiction books). Likewise, the keywords I had put into the back end of Amazon either weren't profitable or weren't keywords at all.

So I started giving thought to what the book was about. After some research we came up with the keywords: self-empowerment, self-esteem, and self-confidence. I then changed the title to reflect some of the keywords that I found to be profitable. Once the keywords were added to the title, the sales began to increase. It was like magic!

With that being said, had we added the keywords into the title from the very beginning we would have had far more success. Also, had we added the keywords to the title and the subtitle, we would have had way more visibility on Amazon. So let's look at an example of how this would look:

Running: A Beginner's Guide To Run Faster & Stronger

In this example, the keywords are running, a beginner's guide, and run faster.

I know these are the keywords because I've plugged them into Amazon's search bar and they've either shown up in the drop down menu or several titles include these keywords in their title.

If you're a non-fiction writer, it's imperative that you include keywords in your title (and if at all possible make them the first few words of your title). To further extend your reach, you want to include keywords in your subtitle as well.

If you are a fiction writer, a creative title is much more common. However you can give yourself a boost in exposure by including keywords in your subtitle.

For example, your title could be The Backwoods (A Mystery Thriller).

In this example, you see that you have your creative title, but you've included your keywords in the subtitle. So when Amazon is pulling back relevant results for the keyword mystery thriller, your book will show up.

Your title is the first place Amazon looks when deciding the relevancy of your book. This is where they give first priority! So let's say your book is a cookbook, yet you have not included cookbook in your title, you've limited that first exposure Amazon provides to books that have the keyword in the title.

If you have a catchy title like Pull Your Pants Up, unless someone is actually searching for these keywords (which in our case many people weren't), your book won't show up in very many results.

So take time with crafting your title and make sure that you have crafted a title that not only captures what your book is about, but also a title that contains one or more keywords.

One last word of caution, I've coached many writers who were so attached to their book title idea that they wouldn't change it. Let me ask you a question. If you had a choice between making little to no money with a book title you love or a book title that contains one or two keywords that could make you a lot of money, which would you choose?

How Book Covers Help Market Your Book

Did you know that your book cover is one of the most important aspects of your book aside from great content? Don't believe the adage, "Don't judge a book by its cover!" Consumers absolutely do judge a book by its cover! It's for that reason that you should take the designing of your book cover seriously.

Make sure you have a professional looking book cover design. It should have a great picture that relays the message of your book, a legible font, and the book cover needs to be eye catching and engaging both as a full size image and as a thumbnail. Your book cover should be able to compete with other books within your niche and be just as eye-catching as the other book covers within its category.

Unless you are a celebrity, household name, or very recognizable public figure you should always steer clear of having your picture on the front of your book cover. Instead, include a professional headshot along with your bio and include it on your back cover if you are publishing a print version of your book.

The most important thing as it relates to book covers, is that they must be professional. I can't stress this enough! If you have a book cover that looks like it was prepared in MS Word, readers are going to skip over your book. They are never going to give it a chance and all of your hard work will be in vain.

You want a book cover that is not only professional, but also one that looks as good as your competition. So it's for that reason that I encourage you to go and look at your competition's book covers. What colors do they use? What kinds of images are they using? What fonts are being used?

For example, I have a client who is finishing up a book about natural hair. When she hired me to do the research on covers, I noticed that almost all of the bestsellers used the color purple on the cover somewhere. This is obviously a common color for this type of book, so why would we change the formula if other writers have already found success?

Conversely, I've also had some of my clients who have been rigid in wanting to change their covers. Either because they already had a cover idea in mind or they didn't want to change a cover that wasn't working well.

Book covers can be a sensitive subject with writers. I believe this happens because we begin to visualize our covers even while we're writing. Because of this, I believe we get stuck on what we have as an idea and don't keep ourselves open to exploring other options.

My first book, *The Buzz*, had a professionally done cover made by one of the premier book cover designers in the industry. He did an excellent job. However, when I released my book seven years ago, while I knew that it needed to be professional, I didn't realize how important it was to have books that were in the same vein as other books within the genre.

While the cover was definitely professional, the colors were too light and playful as it related to the genre I was targeting. And to be honest with you, I liked my cover so much; it took a while before I decided to take my own advice. Again, when we love our covers, it's difficult to change them!

When I looked at the books within my book's genre, the covers were dark, had fancier glittery fonts, and the images were grittier. My book was very light in color with a more playful font. But think about it... if a reader is looking for something gritty, are they going to click on my book or the book with the dark colors and grittier images?

The point I'm trying to make is, sometimes even the most professional book covers don't work, and as writers we have to be open to changing them. I invested a great deal of money in my original cover, but guess what, if a book cover change is all it takes to go from not selling to selling, would you be willing to do it? I know I sure was. So change my book cover I did.

With that being said, spend a decent amount of money on your cover, but don't spend hundreds of dollars. In the event, that you do find yourself having to change your cover in the future, it'll be much easier to make a decision to change the cover if you haven't spent a lot of money.

There are a lot of places you can find professional looking covers. If you are looking for pre-made covers, (covers that are already designed), Google your genre and the words "pre-made." That will pull back a ton of results that will keep you busy for a while. You can also check out sites like http://upwork.com, http://freelancer.com, or even http://fiverr.com.

If I could offer any advice as it relates to getting a book cover designed, make sure you have some idea of how you want your book cover to look. Again, look at your competition and the common fonts, colors, and images used. Present these ideas to your designer and look at their portfolio to determine whether they will be able to provide you with the quality you seek. Once you get your proof back, if there's something you don't like about it, speak up! Your book sales depend on it!

How Book Descriptions Help Market Your Book

Once your perfectly crafted title helps your book to show up in relevant search results and a potential buyer is enticed by your book cover, the next thing they will look at is your book description. In addition to your book cover and title, your Amazon book description is another important factor that determines whether or not your book will do well.

Your book description should read like sales copy. If writing sales copy is not your strong point, hiring someone to write it might not be a bad idea, as your book description is one of the factors readers use to determine if a book is for them.

Within your description you should explain whom the book is for, how the book will help them, and any bragging rights you may have. For example: Featured on the Today Show, #1 Best Seller, New York Times Best Seller, 20,000 copies sold! If you are including bragging rights, lead with it in your description!

Avoid big blocks of text and instead use short sentences and bullet points. Above all, end with a call to action. For example if your book is about health, your call to action could be: Download today and regain your health!

In conclusion, everything mentioned in this chapter can be tweaked at any given point to stimulate sales. As a matter of fact, I encourage you to set up a regular schedule where you're actively looking on Amazon to see what page your book falls on in the categories you've selected, and what pages your book shows up on for the keywords you've selected.

If you find that your book isn't ranking well, then you can make changes one at a time to discover what is hindering your book sales.

For instance, at first you may change your pricing. If that doesn't work, then you may tweak your title. If that doesn't work, you can update your book description. If that doesn't work you may have to go back to the drawing board and revamp your cover.

Whatever you decide to change, give it time to work. Deciding the very next day that your changes didn't help is probably a bad idea. I spoke to an Amazon representative who suggested that authors give their changes three to four weeks to gain traction. I'm still testing out this theory, as it seems you can know within one or two weeks whether your changes are helping or hindering sales.

In conclusion, what has been covered in this chapter might not seem like it relates to book marketing at all, but it does. Each of these elements has an effect on whether your book gets visibility, and once it does get visibility, it effects whether a potential reader buys your book.

To be honest - I have found this part of the process to be more formulaic than creative, so keep that in mind when you begin marketing your book.

The last thing that I want to make clear before we move on to traditional book marketing, is everything mentioned in this chapter is largely dependent on how well you monitor your books. The moment you stop watching your keywords and categories is the moment that another book can swoop in and send your sales rank plummeting. And it's for this reason, that this step is the most important.

What we've discussed in this chapter is your foundation. So don't just do this step and stop. Instead, choose a few of the other book marketing methods that we'll discuss in the coming chapters! Keep an eye on your books, monitor your keywords and categories regularly, utilize some of the book marketing tactics I am going to discuss in the preceding chapters, and watch your sales grow.

Now that we've got that out of the way, let's talk about how you can take your perfectly set up book and turn it into a success!

CHAPTER SEVEN

WHAT ARE YOUR GOALS AS A WRITER?

Your goal may be to have the success of a well-known author like Dean Koontz, to be featured by Oprah as she announces your book as one of her favorites, or maybe you're okay with local notoriety. Whatever your goal, there is no right or wrong answer; it's a personal choice that can only be decided by you.

Outside of writing a great book, marketing is the most important part of the publishing process.

If you are fortunate to be signed to a publishing company that assists in your marketing endeavors, that's wonderful! Be grateful for the help! Working closely with your publisher will boost your own marketing efforts and allow you to reach your goals sooner! What's outlined in this book will be in addition to what your publisher has planned for you.

If you are solely responsible for your marketing, be very specific in your goals and how you will accomplish them. At least one social media platform should be a part of your plan because of its ability to be shared easily with others.

If possible, the marketing of your book should begin when you first have the idea, whether its fiction or non-fiction.

Seth Godin, a book-marketing guru, said in an interview, "The best time to start marketing is a year and a half before you need to sell your book."

If that statement sounds insane to you, then I'm glad you're reading this.

Readers are purchasing more than a book. They are buying into YOU the author, especially in a time where social media makes it easy for us to share and communicate with our audience. In other words...transparency is encouraged!

Determine what makes you stand out as an author! Is it your voice as a writer or your book's subject matter?

There are millions of romance novels flooding the book market, what makes yours stand out? Once you've determined what that "something" is, how will you present it to your target audience?

Your readers want and appreciate a personal connection, so create a community around your audience.

Prior to releasing my book I had a generous fan base of people who followed my blog or knew of me through my freelancing work. Here's what I learned from my early days of social media:

(1) Social media is not just a numbers game – By sheer ease, you can accumulate hundreds or even thousands of followers on social media in a relatively short amount of time. I know because I did it on all of my social media sites! But when it was time to release my book, I discovered the importance of quality over quantity. Meaning, it didn't matter how many people befriended me if those same "friends"

weren't engaged or interested in hearing about my book at some point.

(2) Engage with your audience – Share your writing process, how your husband and kids interrupt your writing time, or something relevant to the topic of your book. The relationship you create with your audience will later influence them to purchase; otherwise they have no real motivation to buy.

With that said, does a successful marketing campaign mean increased sales? I'd love to definitively say yes, but truthfully it doesn't always garner a sale.

Sometimes your marketing will create something intangible like raised awareness for you the author, traffic to your blog, attention on social media, increased views of your videos/book trailers, book reviews, and media requests.

Whether it's an actual sale or one of the opportunities mentioned above, in my opinion they are all equally valuable!

There are many people who will tell you how they sold thousands of copies of their book in a year. I know because I ran into many of these people after releasing my first book. What some of these writers aren't sharing is how they had to consistently market their title.

I often give the example of an unsigned artist. If an independent artist tried to sell you his CD for $5, would you buy it?

Even at such a low price most people will politely decline. Why? They've never heard of the artist. They don't know what the quality of the product is. They don't know if he's any good as an artist. He's not signed to a major record label and the list goes on and on.

Now put that same artist on a social media site...

He's consistently posting new music. You find that it's good quality and the production is good. You've viewed his pictures, read his personal blogs about his passion for music, and he shares that he realized he wanted to be a musician at the age of five when his father first placed a guitar in his hands. He posts the picture to prove it. Later, he posts that he's offering his debut CD for $5.

Now you've gotten to know him a little better. You have an idea of the quality of his music and you understand what drives him as an artist. You are more likely to purchase his CD because he's engaged you! That is the engagement you need with your readers!

The Rule of Seven is an old marketing adage. It says that a prospect needs to see or hear your marketing message at least seven times before they take action and buy from you.

If a buyer needs to see your message seven times before they act, then one interaction on social media promoting your book is not enough. So if someone tells you they sold thousands of copies of their book, a lot of hard work went into it.

From my experience, readers want to know YOU as a writer. And this is especially true for new authors. A catchy title and a nice cover won't be the only thing to persuade someone to buy your book, especially in a sea of books.

But what if... you invited your target market in when you began writing your manuscript. You explained the highs and lows, the writer's block, the interruptions from family, the rewrites and the plot issues. Once you go to print you explain how nervous you are about your first book signing. Will anyone show up? What if only two people come?

Now your audience is emotionally invested. They've been there with you since the beginning. They want to see you succeed and read the final product.

To be clear all of this can be done through any social media site. It's how you decide to use these sites that determines your success.

So take a few minutes and think about your immediate goals and how you will engage your target audience. Brainstorm ways that you can engage your audience based on your book's subject matter.

CHAPTER EIGHT

WHAT IS YOUR COMFORT LEVEL?

You may be wondering, "Stefanie, whatever do you mean what is my comfort level?"

Are you comfortable doing book signings? Radio and television interviews? Marketing your book on social media? Are you comfortable participating in book club meetings?

What about a book release party? Live video streaming? Vending at events? Vlogging? Or attending book festivals?

Are you comfortable starting your own blog? Or contacting magazines for publicity?

What you're comfortable doing will help determine which marketing tactics to employ to accomplish your goals.

I won't argue which marketing strategies I feel are best for authors, because what works for me may not be as successful for you or vice versa. I don't subscribe to the theory that one size fits all, but by assessing your comfort level, you are positioning yourself far better than someone who tries every marketing tactic.

I've had many authors ask me for suggestions on how to market their title. My first question is always, "Are you on social media?" And I am normally met with the response, "Oh no, I'm not a social media or Internet person."

Much of your success and fan base will be found on the Internet because of the ease of sharing and its ability to go viral.

While I am in favor of authors doing what feels comfortable, if you're not an "Internet person" I strongly encourage you to rethink that decision.

Once you sell your book to your friends and immediate family, you need to continue to market your book.

If you're a new author, your challenge is to get readers that aren't familiar with you to purchase your book. If you are an established author, you will be constantly looking for new readers to discover your books. Social media is by far the easiest way to target your audience!

Imagine millions of people standing behind your computer. Some of those people aren't going to be interested in your book, but as you move those uninterested people to the side, those interested readers will step to the forefront. They find you!

How do I know? Because you've found this book sprinkled among all of the others available and I'm ever so grateful to you!)

Publishing is changing. I learn of new authors through social media – and I buy their books! And I tell my friends to buy their books too!

What are your goals as a writer and in what ways are you comfortable marketing to your audience? Now ask yourself, can you logically meet your goals without the Internet?

CHAPTER NINE

GETTING STARTED ON YOUR MARKETING PLAN

A marketing plan is a lot like a business plan. It outlines what your marketing goals are and what tactics you will utilize to accomplish those goals.

Your marketing plan can be created in Microsoft Word (or any other word processing program). It simply needs to document your goals and the steps you will take to achieve them.

Now that you've had an opportunity to assess your goals and comfort level we can now create a realistic marketing plan that you can achieve.

Marketing is an arduous process and by setting realistic goals and achieving them, you can quickly see the fruits of your labor while building a fan base and readership that will help you achieve your bigger goals. My only request - do what works for you!

I can't stress this enough. As you read through this, you are reading an account of how I did things. What I did may or may not work for you. How others market their title may or may not work for you. Create your own marketing plan and decide what will work best for your title.

I'm telling you this because I see a lot of authors get discouraged when they are unable to duplicate the success of another author.

Do what feels comfortable to you! Work in your comfort zone at first, but be open to change. Consistently assess your marketing plan to determine if changes need to be made, but market on your own terms! Your marketing plan should consist of strategies you can realistically achieve.

If your six-month marketing plan consists of: blogging, utilizing all of the social media sites, a book tour, soliciting publicity, and you're working a full-time job while writing a second book, that is not a realistic goal! Provided you're doing all of this alone…

What can you reasonably accomplish in the next six months?

Once you determine what you can accomplish within a six-month period, I encourage you to take the time to get familiar with your book! You'll need to know your book in order to market it. By knowing your book you're prepared to:

Market

Pitch

Be Interviewed

Questions to ask yourself while creating your marketing plan:

- Who is your target audience?

- Is any of your target audience already engaged? Even if only friends and family?
- What does it take to keep your audience engaged?
- Where does your target audience spend their time on the Internet? In real life?
- What do they read? What shows do they watch?
- How are they motivated to purchase?

Once you've created your marketing plan and outlined how you want to market yourself and your title, you may need to revise it from time to time.

Sometimes its necessary to revamp your marketing plan if you're not comfortable with a particular marketing strategy. Maybe it requires more time than you're willing to invest, or it's not providing the results you thought it would.

I created my marketing plan months before the release of my debut novel. There were many components to my plan and social media was at the forefront. After a few months of marketing my title I realized blogging would also be a good marketing strategy.

Remember, a marketing plan is not set in stone! As interest in your book grows and book sales increase, your time and focus changes.

For example, the amount of time you spend in the beginning getting followers on social media, won't be as important once you have thousands who seem to be really tuned in to what you are saying.

You can then focus your time and energy elsewhere. It's for these reasons you should view your marketing plan often to determine if changes need to be made.

A marketing plan is really just a work in progress. Don't think of it, as the end all be all! I've revamped my marketing plan a few times and will continue to do so as my goals are accomplished. Being able to adapt to change has helped me tremendously throughout this process.

If you're a new writer, be prepared to tweak your marketing plan as your buzz grows. If you're an established author, it may be time to pull out the old marketing plan, dust it off and come up with a few new ideas to market your already published books.

It's never too late! Do you know how big the Internet is? There's always someone who hasn't read your book, but is willing to.

CHAPTER TEN

THE PRESS RELEASE

The press release will be the backbone to your marketing plan. It will be used to gain publicity, attract your target market, and so much more.

Personally, I don't believe in recreating the wheel, so if you've already written a synopsis or the spiel for the back cover of your book, you've almost finished your press release. How's that for simple?

Your press release incorporates your marketing angle, so use your creativity to capture the attention of your intended audience with a catchy title and a spiel that persuades them to review your title or feature you.

The key components of a good press release are:

- Targeting your intended audience
- A clear and concise message
- Ideally one page, two pages at the most
- A marketing angle
- Details of your book (ISBN, book dimensions, price, number of pages, etc.)
- Contact information (website and email address)

Consumers are influenced to make purchases based on publicity. Publicity can come in the following ways:

- Newspaper or magazine features
- Interviews
- Television appearances
- Blog or book reviews

It's no easy task to catch the attention of the media. As a freelance writer I receive quite a few queries a day and the press releases that grab my attention have a catchy title, material worth reviewing and a strong marketing angle.

What information does your book provide that will be useful to a media outlet's audience?

Here are some things to note when creating a press release:

- Format your press release and save it as a PDF (if possible)
- Capture attention with a catchy title
- Know your marketing angle(s)
- Press releases can be faxed or emailed, choose one!
- Create more than one press release

Press releases can be put on your website, sent to those in the media, shared on social media, sent to bloggers, and submitted to free press release sites. The whole point is to get the word out about your book!

CHAPTER ELEVEN

GARNERING PUBLICITY FOR YOUR TITLE

We're going to focus on newspaper, magazines, and television as viable ways to garner publicity for your title. Radio is not grouped with the others because it's actually considered advertising.

Traditional radio stations charge advertising fees. So as an alternative, Internet radio is a suitable and sometimes better option as websites like Blogtalkradio.com or podcasts allow you to search for radio shows based on subject matter.

If your book is about relationships, seek out Internet radio shows that discuss relationships. Internet radio hosts are always looking for interesting guests. Make sure your book relates to their show and prepare yourself for the interview by knowing your book!

Whether you are querying newspapers, magazines, television, or Internet radio, the process is the same.

Open an email account. Make sure the account is dedicated strictly to publicity. You want to check this account frequently, so as never to miss an opportunity. Once the email is set up, make sure it has an email signature that includes your website and links to your social media. Ideally your email should be publicity@yourwebsite.com.

Decide which media outlets relate to your book and then search for their contact information on their website or social media profiles.

If the recipient accepts attachments, attach the PDF version of your press release to the email. If your recipient does not accept attachments, you will need to copy and paste the press release to the body of the email. (Keep in mind the formatting might change.)

If your press release is an attachment, include a quick spiel on your book. And I do mean quick!

If you get a reply, respond promptly. Make sure you inquire if anything else is required. (i.e., review copy, headshot, book cover, etc.)

Once you've been interviewed or featured, sit back and enjoy your press! But don't sit too long! Make sure your audience is aware of the publicity you've received by sharing it on your website, blog, and any social media sites you belong to.

Create an online media kit of all the press you've received. Here are some things to note.

- Refrain from adding the media to newsletter mailing lists without their permission.
- If you don't receive a response, move on to another media outlet. Resist the urge to continue to email or spam. Their non-response is because they're uninterested in reviewing your title at this

time. Be careful not to cause a media outlet to lose interest in considering your next book.

- Focus on the relationship. If you are able to secure publicity, nurture the relationship you've created by staying in contact and being of value!
- Say thank you! This is a given, but you should always send an email thanking anyone who has taken the time to read your book and promote it to their audience.
- Always have review copies available. You will give a lot of books away!
- The media sometimes request professional headshots, so be prepared to supply one if necessary!
- Some media outlets will request your book and not follow up for a review, interview, or article. And that's okay! Think of it as the cost of doing business!
- Some outlets will request two copies of your book so that others within their office can review your book too.

Publicity takes time. It may take months before your feature goes to print. Be patient and don't pester your media contact for updates. Do follow up, but consider the lapse of time before doing so. Unless the print date has passed, its unlikely they've forgotten you.

Think outside the box when garnering publicity for your book. If your favorite blog caters to your book's subject matter, email them! National newspapers, magazines, and television shows are all fair game!

While publicists clearly have an advantage because of their established relationships, that has never hindered me from trying to get exposure for my books.

I query any media outlet I feel is a good fit for my book, whether they are a major outlet or small. In some cases, I receive a response, and sometimes I don't so much as hear a peep in return. But... the times I am successful, it is definitely worth it!

I'm sure you've heard the saying; nothing beats a try but a failure. Well you'll never know who is willing to give you publicity if you don't try.

So go for it! Publicity demonstrates the respect that others have for your book. How many times have you purchased an author's book that was featured on television? Or in a magazine? Or on a radio show? Who are you willing to query for publicity?

CHAPTER TWELVE

TRADITIONAL MARKETING FOR WRITERS

There are many strategies authors can employ that won't require social media. I've compiled a list. Most of these will be self-explanatory, however I will provide clarification for some.

- Word of mouth
- Book signings/book release parties
- Book festivals
- Newsletter mailing lists

Aside from what we discussed in chapter one, a newsletter mailing list is arguably the most important book-marketing tactic to employ.

As you go about marketing your book, you will come in contact with potential readers at book signings, book festivals, on social media, your website, and various other places.

These are going to be people who have demonstrated an interest in your writing either by previously purchasing a book, visiting your website or blog, or by adding you on one of their social media accounts.

If you have people that have already shown interest in your books, why recreate the wheel? By capturing their email address, you can further engage with your audience and make them aware of upcoming books. This way every time you release a new book you don't have to go out and find your target audience all over again.

Years ago, just asking for an email address was sufficient. However, things have changed and getting a person to give you their email address is almost like asking them for their credit card number.

So now, writers are creating something of value and giving it to readers for free in exchange for their email address. For example, if you provide me with your email address, I'll send you a free copy of my Book Marketing Timeline. This timeline will share exactly what you need to be doing and when! I've gotten nothing but a positive response from writers in the throes of book marketing about how valuable my timeline is. As a result, I get new subscribers everyday where I further provide them with additional book marketing tips and strategies.

If you are a fiction writer there are several things of value that you can provide. Perhaps you could give away a short story, a preview to your book, or an alternate ending.

For non-fiction writers, it can be a short eBook, a fun giveaway like a Kindle or an iPad, whitepaper, or an exclusive video. Be creative, but above all make sure that it provides value and it's something of interest to your target audience.

Once you've gotten them on your mailing list, update them on upcoming events and books. Share pieces of your personality and be engaging! Eventually you will grow a very substantial list that will be useful to you in the future.

There is great value in your email list as it puts you in direct communication with your audience. If for some unfortunate reason any of your social media sites go away, having access to a reader's email addresses will make the difference in further communication or not. Try to send out an email at least 2-3 times a month to keep your mailing list engaged.

Having the email address of your readers allows you to contact them without restriction. There aren't any algorithms keeping you from showing up in their newsfeed, there is no risk of your profile being banned, and it allows you to connect with your audience on a more personal level.

Personal website

Choose whether your blog or personal website will be the centralized location where you communicate with your audience. I would recommend you have at least one site to send all of your traffic to. Add a way for people to join your mailing list and if you decide for example to sell the print version of your book on your website, provide an incentive. That incentive could be a bookmark or an autographed copy. However, remember, Amazon is usually going to be a buyer's first choice, so if you want them to buy from your website, give them a great reason!

If this is too much for you to maintain, then consider buying a domain name and redirecting it to your Amazon Author Central page. So essentially this means you would buy the domain http://JaneDoe.com and then redirect it to your Amazon Author Central page. Another alternative is purchasing a domain name that contains the keywords surrounding your book's niche and redirecting it to your Amazon Author central page. For example, I own the domain http://howtowriteabookthatsells.com

Email Signatures/business cards

Add your social media sites and personal website to your email signature and business cards. Provide the places where people can find you. This helps you to further grow your network.

Support and network with other writers

Support other writers by visiting their blogs, commenting on their social media, and attending their events. Not only are you increasing your presence, but you are also providing support to someone who is likely looking to increase his or her presence too. Supporting each other only benefits the both of you! Where possible, link up with other authors and create book bundles and help each other to market. Remember, there is power in numbers!

Vending opportunities

Consider vending at local expos, festivals, or community events. Purchase a table at an event marketed towards your target audience.

Book club reviews and meetings

Sit down with a book club in your area to discuss your book. This creates a local following and offline presence. If you are unable to visit with a local book club, solicit online book clubs and ask for a review that can be posted on Amazon, their website, or on social media.

These are just a few traditional book marketing ideas to get you started. In time you will spot new opportunities to sell your book outside of the Internet. Take advantage of any opportunities that will yield results. Be unconventional and take risks! You have nothing to lose!

CHAPTER THIRTEEN

BLOGGING AND THE AUTHOR

Since 2005 when I started freelancing, I've run a blog. It was through having a daily blog I realized that it takes a lot of time and dedication for it to be successful, so blogging was not a part of the first draft of my marketing plan. Initially I felt it would require too much of my time and with launching a company, I felt my time would be best spent elsewhere.

Yet every book marketing article was telling me to blog...

Why blog? Blogs allow authors a centralized place to brand and market themselves. Blogging allows you to have a voice and be an authority on whatever topic you're passionate about. Blogs establish loyalty and drive your target audience to your site every single day.

After understanding how blogging could become a useful part of my marketing plan, I started a blog focused around my writing. Blogging provided a place online where I could share my journey as an author and, because I was providing this information to authors over the phone and in person anyway, well it just made sense.

Should every writer blog? Not necessarily. It's a great way to provide readers with a sampling of your writing and to engage with them well in advance of the release of your book, but it's unlikely that it's perfect for everybody.

Blogging experts suggest you blog consistently (five days a week) and this is why most writers opt against blogging, and the reason why I did too.

However, I'm glad I kept at it. TheWriteOneBlog.com readership has steadily increased over time.

If you decide to blog, consider who you're writing for. Who is your audience and what would you need to talk about consistently in order to keep them engaged? For instance, my target audience is writers. So I consistently talk about book marketing and publishing in order to keep my readers coming back day after day.

Once you've determined who you're blogging for, remember to share openly and honestly. Your readers will appreciate your authenticity. Blogging tends to attract an authentic voice, so getting started should be relatively simple.

Remember that blogs are a two-way conversation with the reader. By monitoring your blog's comments and responding, you'll create an engaged audience and you'll find new ideas to blog about from that daily interaction.

When starting your blog have foresight! Have a clear idea of the focus and remember that you will be writing future books and they may have different subject matters.

TheWriteOneBlog.com is "The Author's Guide To Book Publishing, Book Marketing & More!"

Last but not least, have fun with your blog! There are no rules. Your only objective is to keep your readers engaged. So give it some thought…do you think you have time to blog? And what will you blog about?

CHAPTER FOURTEEN

WRITERS AND SOCIAL MEDIA

Before I discuss using social media as an author, please make yourself familiar with all of the different social media platforms. I won't speak on any one particular social media site because they are ever changing. There are pros and cons to all social media platforms and I'm not here to endorse one over the other, only to encourage you to figure out which platform works best for you.

What I will provide is how to effectively market on these sites as a writer. But first let's start with what not to do on social media!

Using Social Media Correctly

Social media is a loud and overcrowded scene. No matter which social media platform you choose - make yourself stand out! It should be said that standing out is not always accomplished by doing or saying something outrageous, but instead by providing value!

If you wrote a book about parenting, then I absolutely expect to find you on social media speaking to parents, homeschool moms, single moms, first time moms, and anyone that can relate to your book. I expect to see parenting tips, funny stories about your experiences as a mother, and pictures of your kids. Remember you are not just on social media to promote, promote, promote!

Self-promotion will only prove to be an annoyance to your followers. Instead, provide tips, share articles, and share engaging stories. If people are connected to you on social media, they have access to your profile and they will know you are a writer. If what you are sharing is of value, believe me, they will seek out your books, your website, and your other social media profiles.

Now this is not to say you should never promote your book. You absolutely should! But you should not make marketing your book your only way of communicating on social media. Eventually people will bypass your posts and move on to someone who's using social media correctly.

Here are a few tips for writers using social media:

- Decide whether you will use your personal account for attracting your target audience or if you will create a page specifically for your writing persona.
- Know your voice on the Internet. Will you be whiny, bratty, the intellect, or the reclusive author? De-pending on your genre, there is value in certain voices.

- Choose your voice wisely. Shy away from using your platform to share all of your gripes. It can be useful depending on your book's subject matter, but use it sparingly. It can easily be annoying!
- Everything you put on the Internet is out there for the world to see for years and years to come, so be mindful of what you share.
- Participate and develop relationships with literary agents, editors, book publishers, and most of all, your readers. After all, they don't call it social networking for nothing!
- Nurture relationships by creating value. People will actively look for and share your posts if you are providing information they can't find anywhere else.
- Link to your website and books in your profile, when possible.
- Promote your events, book signings, and webinars.
- Engage your social media friends in conversation about things related to your book.

How To Be Successful On Social Media

Growing a fan base is a process. There are days when there are just a few new followers and days where waves of people will find you.

During those times you should be looking at your marketing to determine what you've done to create this momentum and if possible continue it.

Social media is a constant conversation and can definitely be considered a time-sink. Before deciding on which social media platforms you will add to your marketing plan, decide if the time required is what you're able to devote.

Remember, social media site isn't a numbers game even though others will make you believe that. While a lot of followers are clearly important for the "big picture," followers who are engaged are more significant!

After all, what good will a lot of followers do you if they aren't listening to anything you say? Start small and create your audience organically!

Social media makes it easier to build a big audience. If a reader shares your book or website with their audience, they just helped you market your book beyond your own personal reach. If you understand how to use social media to your benefit, the only thing needed is an investment of your time.

With that said, take just as much care in choosing who you follow on social media. Remember, you are creating a community. Also observe the types of people who follow you. Are you attracting your target audience or people just looking to increase their count?

If you aren't attracting your target audience, is it because of the content you are sharing? Diversify your posts and make sure you have a varied style of posting. Maybe on one day you can share a motivational quote, the next day ask your audience a question, or share an issue that one of your characters is facing.

Now, how can you add value to your followers? Have you looked at their profile? How old are they? What are their hobbies? What books are they currently reading? Where do they hang out?

When my company, Write One Publications, Inc., joined social media, my focus was in determining my worth and using that worth to not only increase my followers, but most importantly, to have an engaged audience.

I found my niche on social media by sharing my writing journey, giving book marketing and writing tips, posting funny memes and motivational quotes, and sharing links to my blog posts. I have found this extremely helpful in growing my audience across all of my social media platforms. It was not an overnight process and there were days when I absolutely felt like giving up, but when I look back now even though I don't have tens of thousands of followers like other writers, I do have a very supportive bunch.

With that being said, I've compiled a list of three tips that writers can apply now to improve their web presence and find their target audience.

1. Listen and engage in the conversation - Use hashtags (#) to listen to what your audience is discussing. Just about every social media site now takes advantage of hashtags. Don't be afraid to engage in the conversation or provide value to someone looking for tips and advice on a particular subject, especially as it relates to your book's subject matter. Engagement helps you attract new followers and increases traffic to your blog/website and books.

2. Network - Make a good first impression. Welcome your new followers! Take a few minutes, if possible, to view their profile and talk to them. When someone first adds you on social media, that is the perfect time to introduce yourself and network.

3. Use your time wisely - Let's face it, social media can be a time-sink and can draw you away from what you should be doing—writing. If you're good at multi-tasking, jumping on and off social media throughout the day won't seem like too much of a disruption. If it seems like a distraction, determine what time(s) of the day your audience is signed on. I usually sign in three times a day (morning, noon, and early evening).

From my experience, I find that my audience is on first thing in the morning. Midday and evening seems to attract users signing in from their desks or just returning home from work. Knowing this allows me the ability to divvy my time between social media, writing, blogging, and the other responsibilities of my company.

It's also important to note that you should log on more than once a day. Depending on the number of followers of another user, they may or may not see your post. Visiting your social media sites at least twice a day betters your chances! If you can't log on everyday, that's fine! Just make your time count.

Make sure you show your personality by participating in conversations! This is just as important as any post promoting your book.

Above all, have fun! Some of my best laughs come from my social media friends, and it's also where I gain knowledge on an array of topics!

CHAPTER FIFTEEN

FINAL THOUGHTS

Now that you've chosen a few book marketing strategies that will work best for your book, you now have a bare bones marketing plan that can be executed today. There's no financial investment involved except the investment of your time.

Anything you want to achieve as an author is attainable with goal setting and tools by which to achieve it. I sincerely hope that you are now prepared to begin or resume the marketing of your title.

A lot of what I've discussed will take you away from writing itself, so try just a few strategies at a time and be realistic in your goals!

What I've described may sound easy or overwhelming depending on where you currently are in your marketing. Either way, be prepared to be in it for the long haul!

If I could stress anything, it would be to have patience and faith. Know that you are only one person and it takes time to create a following. If you keep on in the manner described in this book, you'll attract readers who will help get the word out about your book. They will, in essence, act as your marketing team.

If this book has enlightened you or provided value in any way, please multiply my efforts by writing a review on Amazon. Assist me in helping another writer be successful in their marketing.

I sincerely hope you've found value in this book! This book was truly a labor of love and something I wanted to share with aspiring writers to encourage them to never give up on marketing their book!

ABOUT THE AUTHOR

Stefanie Newell has earned a stellar reputation as the go-to writing coach for the first time writer who's looking for direction on how to write and publish their first book. Through her writing, publishing, and marketing expertise, she helps aspiring writers to unleash their authentic voice and share their message through the pages of their book. Not only has she assisted beginners in bringing their book idea to fruition, but her expertise has also paved the way for her to coach an accomplished Hollywood film and television producer.

In addition to coaching authors through her How To Write A Book program, Stefanie is also an author.

Her greatest reward however, is assisting her clients in telling their personal stories and fulfilling their goal of becoming a published author.

To learn more about Stefanie's book consulting company, visit her website at www.howtowriteabookthatsells.com.

CPSIA information can be obtained
at www.ICGtesting.com
Printed in the USA
LVOW01s0156191216
517889LV00015B/1092/P